PRAISE AND ENDORSEMENTS

A groundbreaking and important offering! Far too often, women forget to take loving care of themselves, forgoing their needs out of the notion that a good mother is one who sacrifices what nourishes her body, mind, and spirit. In this wise and powerful guide, Suzi Lula reminds us that we shortchange ourselves *and* our children when we neglect ourselves.

Susan Stiffelman
Author of "Parenting Without Power Struggles"
and "Parenting with Presence"

The Motherhood Evolution is a powerful offering from a powerful teacher, sure to help countless women feel liberated from the burdens of guilt, self-abandonment and the sheer exhaustion that is so typical of motherhood. Suzi's wise guide and new vision of motherhood supports mothers to have the relationships they yearn to have with their kids, and to begin living their best lives while raising children to live their best lives as well.

Katherine Woodward Thomas
Author of The New York Times Bestseller "Conscious Uncoupling"
and National Bestseller "Calling in 'The One'"

The Motherhood Evolution shimmers with clarity, love, compassion, and wisdom. Through her crystal-clear prose and counseling clients' heartfelt stories, Suzi brilliantly shifts the mothering paradigm from an outdated duality—my child *or* me, abundance *or* lack, all *or* nothing—into a larger context of motherhood where Self-Care is a spiritual practice that naturally reconnects, revitalizes, and renews our awareness of the Authentic Self, yielding expansive benefits for children, our loved ones, and the world. This is a must-read for mothers, for sure, and for anyone who desires to Awaken and live an Authentic life.

H. Ronald Hulnick, Ph. D.

President, University of Santa Monica and, Co-Author "Loyalty to Your Soul: The Heart of Spiritual Psychology"

With **The Motherhood Evolution**, Suzi Lula has her gentle finger squarely on the pulse of the zeitgeist, where self-care is trending. Lula traces the contours of transformative self-care for mothers, which extends beyond manicures, massages and "me-time" into the realm where true personal – and planetary – evolution is mined. Lula writes, "Mothers are here to change the world. We have the capacity to embrace the shadow. ...When we embrace our own [shadows], we become a powerful force of change within our families, society and the world at large." An important shadow Lula helps mothers illuminate and navigate is so often a key (and usually undiscussed) obstacle to parents seeking peace: unresolved hurts and losses from their own childhoods. *The Motherhood Evolution* shines most brightly when Lula shares inspiring, instructive client case histories in which mothers at any age or stage will find themselves, along with sound ideas for tending soul and spirit.

Marcy Axness, PhD

Author, "Parenting for Peace: Raising the Next Generation of Peacemakers"

Suzi Lula has written a transformational guide to motherhood. In **The Motherhood Evolution**, she shows us that when we feel ourselves to be somehow lacking, our children also tend to grow up believing themselves to be lacking. Suzi teaches us that, as mothers, we are not only worthy as individuals, we bring valuable energy to the world—we are abundant! It was way late in my parenting experience as a mother of two that I learned just how important taking care of "me" first was. **The Motherhood Evolution** is "that book" I wish I had been able to read when I was a mother of young children. Suzi's experience and skills in this field are nothing less than brilliant.

Laurie Lankins Farley
Co-author, "Conversations With God For Parents"
written with **Neale Donald Walsch**

Suzi introduces mothers to a powerful concept ... what if we mother and parent from a place of fulfillment, abundance, and thriving ... what would THAT look like? It would look like **The Motherhood Evolution**! This book is transformative. You'll never look at mothering the same way again!

Johanna Maaghaul
Waterside Productions

Suzi Lula has a unique capacity to share deep truths and transformational insights within a light, user-friendly context. Her words flow with an open heart, lovingly embracing and encouraging us to explore what it means to thrive as a mother and a global peace ambassador. **The Motherhood Evolution** and it's timely, revolutionary message quenches the profound thirst that mothers everywhere have to finally thrive.

Judy Julin
Publisher of Inspired Parenting Magazine, founder of CosmiKids and CEO of Engage Enterprises, the lead developer of community-based multi-generational learning centers

Through her advocacy of self-care, Suzi Lula is an expert in helping transform the experience of motherhood. This uplifting and inspiring book offers attainable tools and guideposts for moms to embrace self-care as a first step to tapping into our inner wisdom and building deeper connections with our kids.

Suzi is a voice of change for Mothers everywhere.

Roma Khertapal
Author, "The 'Perfect' Parent"

So many times over the years I've caught myself and my clients worried that they were not good enough. Not good enough mothers, wives, friends, or employees. As women, we run ourselves down until we are on empty. In this revolutionary book Suzi Lula has given a road map to mothers everywhere. She leads us back home to ourselves, where we can nourish our souls and find peace in our body, mind, and spirit.

Michelle Gale
Co-Founder of The Family Awareness Project &
Advisor to the Wisdom 2.0 Conference

Suzi Lula

The Motherhood

Evolution

How Thriving Mothers Raise Thriving Children

The Motherhood Evolution/Suzi Lula — 1st ed.

ISBN 978-1-7359743-4-7 (pbk)
ISBN 978-1-7359743-5-4 (eBook)

www.SuziLula.com

CONTENTS

Acknowledgments 11

Foreword by Dr. Shefali Tsabary 12

Introduction by Dr. Michael Bernard Beckwith 14

Introduction For Mothers to Thrive is to Change the World 17

1   From Self-Sacrifice to Self-Care 20

2   What Your Child Really Wants—and What *You* Really Want, Too 28

3   Self-Care Isn't for the Faint of Heart. 39

4   The Martyred Mother 44

5   Guilt—the Martyr's Cousin 51

6   Mutuality—Of Mutual Benefit. 59

7   Abundance Is Your Birthright. 65

8   More than Enough. 69

9   Who Are You Really? 77

10 A View from the Mountaintop 85

11 The Emotional Messenger System 91

12 Connection. 105

13 The Field of Motherhood 115

14 Make Friends with the Universe 122

15 From Ego to Essence 131

16 Self-Care as a Spiritual Practice 143

17 Invest in Yourself. 152

18 Mothers Who Meditate. 161

19 Practices that Will Enrich Your Life. 168

20 How Good Can Your Life Be? 185

21 A Global Sisterhood of Thriving Mothers 191

22 Living in the House of Tomorrow 196

Full Circle Moment 205

To Jami and William, my wings

When my father taught me to drive, he told me never to let my tank go below half full .... how right he was!

ACKNOWLEDGMENTS

Infinite gratitude for my best friend and soul-mate, Jami, and my joy-filled, exuberant son and greatest teacher, William. More love and support I can't imagine receiving.

Kristen Perkins and Chelsea Field, better friends and mothers just don't exist!

Michael Bernard Beckwith and my Beloved Agape Community, I'm me because of you. Dr. Shefali Tsabary, mother-sister-friend doing conscious parenting work of the highest order, you inspire me beyond measure. David Robert Ord, editor extraordinaire, your artful crafting has made my words shine!

To every client I've ever worked with, I've learned so much from each of you. To every friend who has heard me talk about this book, thank you for holding it in your heart until I could hold it in mine.

To every mother who may be struggling to make it through the day, or seeking to live a more meaningful, purposeful, inspired and fulfilled life, may this book find you. To every mother on the planet ready to join together in sacred sisterhood, may we find each other.

And finally, to Julia Padawer, I can't thank you enough. This book simply wouldn't exist without you.

FOREWORD BY

Dr. Shefali Tsabary

The *Motherhood Evolution* is foundational for all mothers. Suzi Lula has written a once-in-a-lifetime book that will free mothers from the cultural shackles of martyrdom, lack, and self-sacrifice that we have accepted for so long as the norm, and guide them toward an entirely new perspective of motherhood—one of abundance, wholeness and worth. This is one of those rare books that has the potential to irrevocably change your life and the way we view motherhood as a society.

In my own counseling of parents during the course of many years, like Suzi I've found that countless mothers run on empty. Consequently they are exhausted, frustrated, and frequently upset with both themselves and their children—a state that then compounds their guilt about not being "good enough" as a mother. And, also like Suzi, I've learned that it doesn't have to be this way. If you're struggling with feeling worn down, or you are experiencing a lack of meaning in your life now that your children occupy so much of your attention, this book is a sure guide to finding fulfillment as an individual, while at the same time mothering in a manner that's optimal from the point of view of your child's needs.

This powerful book offers inestimable wisdom on how to shift motherhood from "running on empty" to a state of overflowing fulfillment and joy. It provides a sturdy guide to nourish your spirit, feed your soul, and create an empowered connection with your children. In the process, it assists you in unpacking the emotional baggage that inhibits an intimate connection with your children. If you allow this book to guide you, your relationship with yourself, your children, and everyone in your life will be transformed.

Asking the pivotal question, "What if we begin to view the whole of motherhood through the filter of abundance rather than lack?" invites us to usher in a new vision of motherhood that will transform us as mothers, as leaders in our families and consequently, the world.

Suzi brings in her decades-long experience as a counselor, along with the lessons learned from her personal journey of discovering her intrinsic worth as both a human being and a mother.

I cannot recommend this book highly enough.

Shefali Tsabary, PhD

New York Times Bestselling Author of *The Conscious Parent*

INTRODUCTION BY

Dr. Michael Bernard Beckwith

Suzi Lula has served for many years as an esteemed colleague, trans-formational teacher in our University and as a highly sought after licensed spiritual counselor at The Agape International Spiritual Center, the community I founded. It is in her son, William, where I observe the results of her personal application of the principles of visionary mothering she shares in this book. I have deliberately chosen the word "visionary" as a precise description of Suzi's profound contribution, because even in our postmodern times it is taken for granted that when a woman assumes the role of mother it goes arm-in-arm with self-sacrifice. As Suzi highlights, segments of our society consider it a moral imperative that mothers surrender their personal and spiritual needs to the demands of motherhood. This creates within them a climate of guilt, blame, and shame. And as Suzi astutely points out, *a mother's inner climate becomes the overarching climate of her children's lives.*

Motherhood is, in and of itself, a path of personal awakening, for it begins when a woman births within her consciousness an honoring of the precious gift of her own life. Out of this sacred acknowledgment there arises a realization that the more she nurtures her self-development, the more skillful she will be in nourishing the children she births. The art of mothering from a wise place of balancing self-care with childcare is not about self-sacrifice, a martyrdom of oneself, but rather the joy that arises from true giving that is born of inner self-fulfillment.

As I read the wisdom in Suzi's book, I immediately felt the spirit of my own beloved mother, Alice Geneva Beckwith, who made her transition nearly three years ago. A mother of three sons, she was exceptionally ahead of her time when it came to society's prevailing philosophy of raising children back in the 50s. While reading through the pages of the book you hold in your hands, I realized that she applied many of the skillful practices Suzi Kesler Lula emphasizes.

First, she believed that all persons come into this world with a purpose and path unique to themselves. She clearly demonstrated this in her own life by being faithful to herself as an individual, as a woman, a wife, and as a mother who guided and supported each of her sons to become their authentic selves.

Secondly, in the 60s, our dear mother answered a deep inner call to social activism. By living the principles she believed in, she taught us that there exist noble purposes for taking a stand beyond one's immediate family unit and how "family" included the larger world community. As young boys we were aware when she was out picketing, that she was protesting for civil and human rights and we were proud of her. Alice's determination to demonstrate her personal belief in the dignity of all beings continued to impact our lives in tremendously meaningful ways as we became men, husbands, and parents.

Thirdly, as our family grew to include nieces, nephews, and eventually daughters-in-law and grandchildren, we watched Alice balance self-care with devotedly caring for us all. She modeled how to be independent, to foster our individual growth and development, and for this she was greatly loved and respected. Alice proved that the legacy a mother leaves upon departing from this world is not just those to whom she gave birth, but rather that she taught each of her children how to give birth to their own highest potential. Through her daily life on the planet, she showed us by example how taking responsibility for our self-care is at the core of nurturing and supporting the loved ones in our lives.

If the mothers of the world were to come together to honor themselves as women, simultaneously included would be the celebration of their motherhood. When mothers sing, dance, meditate, pray, laugh, and joyfully abide within themselves, they are telling their children that they too have lives worthy of celebration. By following their individual purpose and calling, mothers etch upon the minds of their children that they are fully empowered to cultivate their unique gifts, talents, and skills, and thus honor the purpose for which they have taken a precious human incarnation.

In *The Motherhood Evolution*, real women's voices are heard describing how they really feel. From Suzi Lula they receive generous doses of understanding, compassion, wise guidance, support, and assurance on how empowering the vision they have for their lives as women and mothers can be lived in a most fulfilling way.

How lovingly Suzi offers that same gift to every woman who reads this visionary book.

Michael Bernard Beckwith
Founder, The Agape International Spiritual Center

For Mothers to Thrive is to Change the World

As a wife, mother and spiritual counselor, I've learned that the better I care for *myself*, the better able I am to care for those around me, especially my son. I've learned that this journey of self-care, or inner-care as I call it, is not for the faint of heart. It takes courage and conviction to care for the precious life that we have been given and live the life that we have come here to live. While I've always felt this way and practiced this in my life, it wasn't until having my son that it became vitally important because now my life and the way I live it affects his own precious life.

Simultaneously, in my counseling practice, I've found that mothers everywhere are seeking to live a life overflowing with meaning and purpose. Mothers are the spiritual heart of the family, the spiritual heart of the planet, actually. Mothers experience such a profound spiritual connection when meeting our children for the first time and yet can so easily lose that connection when moving into the "doing" phase of caring for them and end up feeling exhausted, alone, and disheartened—sometimes struggling just to make it through the day. Mothers can experience what I call a sort of spiritual bankruptcy and are yearning to reconnect, mother—and live—from their spiritual center, power and authority. It is for this reason that I've come to know mothers as the untapped spiritual powerhouse of the planet.

Mothers are among the great givers of the world. No one loves and wants more for their children than mothers. Mothers seek to do, arguably the most important work on the planet, more often than not, from an empty tank. In working with mothers over the years, I've come to realize a direct correlation between the ability to carry out this high calling of motherhood—from a place of abundance rather than lack—and the practice of self-care. This has led me to a full on study of and advocacy for mothers to care for themselves and nourish their spirits, that they may give from an overflowing wellspring of well-being, vitality and inexhaustible good.

Those who wear the "hood of the mother," whether a parent, grandparent, teacher or guardian, have the first imprint on our children and therefore, the greatest imprint on society. Yet, motherhood is one of the least valued and most invisible segments of our culture. The entire world of the mother lives largely unnoticed. It's time to bring value to and shine the light on mothers everywhere. Buckminster Fuller—surely a man who made a difference in the world if there ever was one—when asked to define genius responded, "Someone who had the right *mother*."

On a personal note, my own mother, who I know loved me dearly, was also the queen of martyrdom. A product of the depression mentality, she was self-made and quite successful. Yet, she wasn't able to enjoy the fruits of her labor. Instead, she deprived herself to such an extreme that I thought her mentality of severe lack and deprivation was real. Her self-sacrifice came at a high cost, both to her and me.

My mom martyred herself thinking she was doing something *for* me. Many of us martyr ourselves without even really being aware we are doing so. Now, I've learned that you can't deprive your way to a thriving life, especially when you do it "for the sake of the children."

I seek to break the chains, that my son and all children may live liberated. To that end, I wrote the book.

Nourishing our spirits, our inner life, is the single most effective way to create the quality of connection and family life that we are all seeking.

Nourishing our inner life is the most powerful portal to experiencing prosperity, abundance and overflow in our lives. It's not an exaggeration to say that self-care shifts our very experience of motherhood from lack to abundance. Taking the time to care for ourselves feels good! This "good" feeling is the feeling of abundance.

I have a vision of mothers all around the world flourishing: living and giving from this overflowing abundance. I see mothers as the ultimate philanthropists! May you be one of them. I have a vision of mothers all around the world uniting, joining together and evolving our collective vision of what motherhood can be. May your mothering experience be greater than you can possibly imagine. There's a new conversation emerging that raises the roof on what is possible for mothers everywhere—the sky is the limit! May you be part of this emerging conversation of the possibility and potentiality for mothers everywhere!

1

From Self-Sacrifice to Self-Care

Quite out of the blue, my son William walked into my office and handed me a report card he had made from an index card. Inscribed on the card were the words, "Mommy smiling: A+."

At the bottom of my report card he had added a personal note, much like a teacher might do on a report card from school. It read, "Mommy, you are doing a great job of smiling more!"

Mom's Report Card

Smiling = A+

A+

You are doing great!

This comment from my twelve-year-old warmed my heart, and he was right. I had been smiling more. That's because I had been nourishing my spirit, and he felt it.

It had all begun a month earlier when William had commented to me as we drove home from school, "Mom, you really need to smile more. You are always so serious." I felt a dagger pierce my heart. Did my son really think I was too serious? I thought I was pretty cool!

After a deep breath in, I invited, "Tell me more."

"You're serious about everything," he proceeded to inform me. "Like when I get in the car after school, the first thing you want to know is what my plan is for doing my homework. Then you want to know when I'm going to clean my room."

I was about to react, "Well, if you'd clean your room the first time I ask, I would smile more." Thankfully, I caught myself, took another deep breath in, and buttoned my lips. Deep down, something inside me knew he was right, that I was too serious. So I allowed my awareness to reach down into that serious place within me. As I attuned my inner ear to it, I was surprised to hear the "serious" part of me say that *it, too, wanted to smile more.*

"The serious part of me wants to smile more," I repeated to myself. It was quite a realization. In the days that followed, I found myself becoming acutely aware of the severe way I can be with myself. I thought about how I can be so hard on myself, how I can expect so much from myself, and how I can deprive myself of things that feed my soul.

I'm not talking about some great deprivation, just the little ways in which I short-change myself in terms of the things I enjoy. Maybe you do the same, perhaps not even realizing it?

For instance, I might tell myself, "Oh, I'm okay. I don't need to take the time to go all the way to my yoga class." By telling myself this, I brush aside the fact that yoga awakens the vitality within me, connecting me with my heart. The sense of "fullness of being" it enables me to access gets me smiling more not just in my relationship with William, but in the whole of my life, for it awakens the *inner* smile within me.

Because I could hear what my son was saying to me, I created an experiment and embarked upon a journey to "lighten up" on myself. I recommitted to the things I know awaken the life force within me, the things that enliven me, yoga being one of them. Following class, I also began writing at a cafe before seeing clients—something seemingly so simple, but not necessarily so easy for me to give myself permission to carry out.

However, each time I made the effort to care for myself, the results were exponential. My renewed vitality spilled over into a feeling of inner connection I'd been missing, a sense of gratitude and contentment, and a creativity that far outlasted the actual time I spent writing. I noticed how much more patient and lighthearted I was with William when he arrived home from school. I was more the mother I wanted to be—and, more importantly, the mother he needed me to be. The quality of our relationship was richer.

Here's the really interesting question to me. When we know things like yoga, exercise, meditation, or taking a walk are truly beneficial, why do we end up putting them on the back burner? In fact, not only back burner them, but even resist them?

From Sacrifice to Sacred

For many years, my intention has been to live a fulfilled life. Actually, I aim to live an *inspired* life so that I can make my time on Earth a masterpiece.

When I became a mother, this became even more important, for the quality of *my* life now affects the quality of my son's life. Yet now that I had a child, to actually live an inspired life suddenly became much more challenging. I found it quite difficult to engage in the kinds of things that really brought quality to my life.

This was only partly because another being was now entirely dependent on me. Mostly it was because of an unspoken cultural message that says sacrifice is noble, and to even think of considering your own needs alongside of, let alone before, those of your child is to be self-centered.

The idea that "taking care of ourselves is selfish" is a deeply ingrained belief I find myself encountering constantly in the clients, and especially mothers, I see in my counseling practice.

No one loves their child more, wants more for their child, and seeks to give to their child more than a mother. But a mother can't truly give to her child - or anyone else for that matter - when her own tank is empty.

Deep down within us, we intuitively know these things, yet we have such a struggle with taking care of our own needs as mothers. I know that when I finally realized I needed to place my needs not last on my to-do list but ahead of everything else, it initially felt selfish. However, in practice it turned out to be anything but.

There's never been a more important time for mothers to nurture themselves. The better we care for ourselves, the more we flourish—and the more we flourish, the easier it is to consciously care for our children.

Rather than "sacrificing" ourselves for the sake of our children, as has so long been the mother's mantra, we must commit to being *thriving* for the sake of our children. We must dare to say that by putting ourselves first, paradoxically we have *more* to give to our children. And giving that flows from our own fullness, instead of from being run ragged, is done joyously and abundantly.

Ironically, when we serve our family from a sense of overflowing well- being, we restore the word "sacrifice" to its original meaning, which is to "make sacred."

Permission to Thrive

Mothers are doing some of the most important work on the planet, yet they are among the most undervalued segments of society—in many cases almost to the point of invisibility. Consequently, I've found myself becoming somewhat of an advocate for mothers. When mothers flourish, living a life of meaning and purpose, it not only enriches their relationship with their children but every relationship in their life.

Mothers in particular appear to need "permission" to take care of their own needs alongside those of others. They don't seem to realize that they too have not just a need but an inherent *right* to flourish.

I love the word "thrive," which speaks to the experience of an inner sense of well-being in the midst of any external situation we find ourselves in—and that consequently surpasses any fulfillment we can derive from the world around us, or from our children.

To thrive as mothers means we experience a sense of well-being even in the chaos that often closes in around us where raising our children is concerned. If there's one group on the planet whose spirits need to be nourished, and who therefore need desperately to engage in this inner-care, it's mothers.

The announcement heard before every commercial jetliner takes off speaks to us as mothers: "Put your own oxygen mask on *first*."

When we hear this announcement on a flight, we don't think that putting on our oxygen mask first would be selfish. We understand we can best assist others when our own mask is securely in place. Well, just as we value the importance of this act of self-care in an emergency, why wouldn't we value self-care in our daily life?

Thinking that self-care is selfish implies that a mother would take care of herself to the exclusion of her children. Quite the opposite, those with the most vitality are the *first* to assist others in life. When oxygen masks drop from above us on a flight, we don't for a moment intend to put on our own oxygen mask, then do nothing to assist those around us.

None of us wants to be called selfish or, worse, "narcissistic," which is the tendency to imagine the world revolves around us. So it may surprise you to hear that taking care of ourselves is actually the *antidote* to narcissism. How so? In narcissism—and, surprisingly, its polar opposite, feeling like a martyr—our whole focus is ironically on *ourselves*.

When I am running on fumes, without saying a word, I can walk into a room and everyone can feel my grumpy mood. My son may think he needs to walk on eggshells, so as not to "upset mommy." Everything is revolving around me and my mood. *This* is narcissism!

In contrast, when we care for ourselves and take the time to nourish our spirit, our life is enriched and we are able to care for and truly give to others from our overflow.

Caring for ourselves is not only *not* selfish, it's the most self-*less* thing we can do for our children.

Are You Running on Empty?

If you are running on empty, caring for others feels burdensome. In contrast, caring for others when your tank is full and on overflow causes you to feel alive and purposeful. When we are full, we can be completely present with our children and those around us.

In my counseling practice, I notice that mothers especially tend to run on empty. We think of inner-care as expendable. When the pressure is on, caring for her own well-being is usually the first thing tossed from a mother's list.

Ironically, it's precisely when finding time for inner-care seems the most challenging that it's actually most needed and most warranted. These are the moments when self-care should be just about the last thing to go.

Today, more and more mothers are seeking to live their life and parent their children in a more awakened and conscious way. But striving to do this challenging work from an empty tank is virtually impossible. Context is everything. When we change the context from one of lack and deprivation to one of abundance and fulfillment, the whole experience of motherhood itself changes.

When *you* are thriving, all those around you benefit.

Motherhood Through the Lens of Abundance

We have been gifted with life—that of our *own*, not just our child's. The better we treasure and care for this precious life, the better we encourage our children and everyone around us to live meaningful, purposeful, and richly rewarding lives.

This seems so simple, yet the internal pressure we experience, along with the cultural pressure—not to mention the sheer logistics involved when raising children—sometimes makes taking the simplest step of caring for ourselves feel like we're swimming upstream. Constantly battling against a current that says we should "do without" in order to serve our children certainly isn't fun, and neither does it really work—not for us, and not for our children or anyone else around us.

In our culture, I witness what I call a martyr complex and a guilt epidemic. I can't tell you how many women *and* men talk to me about how they somehow feel they're never "doing enough," never "good enough." Thus, the thought of doing what it takes to nourish our spirit, instead of giving all our attention to our children, is seen through a filter of guilt. We then seek to alleviate this feeling by overdoing and overachieving, which never works.

Look closely at this filter and you'll see that it's rooted in an either-or mentality. Such a mindset is based on a belief in lack and implies that if one person gets their needs met, another may not. This causes us to abandon what, deep within ourselves, we *know* to be true for us—that if we don't take good care of ourselves, we can't really take care of anyone else.

But what if there's actually more than enough for everyone to have their needs met, especially our children? And not only met, but met in abundance? What if abundance, not lack is, is the natural way of things?

What if we began to view the whole of motherhood through the filter of abundance rather than lack? What if we looked at motherhood through a filter of *both-and* rather than *either-or*? What if it actually *benefitted* my child when I take care of myself?

Isn't this what philanthropy is all about? A philanthropist has an abundance of good that they graciously share with others. In the same vein, I have a vision of mothers overflowing with inspired energy and enjoying a fulfilling life. Wouldn't we then freely share our vitality with our children and our gifts with the world?

2

What Your Child Really Wants— and What *You* Really Want, Too

When we meet our child for the first time, we are gifted with the most profound relationship between any two humans. But no sooner do we move into the active phase of caring for this child than the deep connection we initially experience seems to vanish. Consequently, many mothers end up feeling disconnected, disheartened, and in many ways alone.

But disconnected from *what?*

As I talk with my clients, I increasingly see how becoming a mother can sometimes so easily disconnect a woman from her very *self.* The reason for this is that we are inclined to allow all the "doing" associated with motherhood to trump the vital importance of approaching motherhood from a sense of *being.*

There is within each of us an incredible fullness of being that yearns to express itself. It's an enthusiasm for life, an excitement, a joie de vivre as the French call it.[1] Disconnected from this overflowing fullness within us, we go through our mothering experience feeling more like an empty tank—and empty tanks can't overflow with purpose, patience, kindness, compassion, and the kind of outpouring of connection and caring on which families thrive. It's because we feel disconnected from

---

[1] Joy of living.

our true self that we often feel detached from our most precious gift, our children.

Now let me ask you to consider something. When you feel a longing inside you, a yearning, have you ever thought of this deep hunger not as an emptiness you somehow need to fill, but as *your own inherent fullness that's just dying to express itself?*

There's a world of difference between an emptiness seeking to be filled and a fullness seeking to pour forth in abundant self-expression. If we don't recognize this, we get just about everything connected with motherhood pretty much backwards.

The truth is, many of us are dying on the vine. Dying on the vine, yes—but far more than that, especially as mothers, we are *dying to live,* to *truly* live. And if we only knew it, the amazing thing is that our children are dying for us to truly live as well.

This is why it's so important to delve into our inner environment, from which we will naturally, be impelled to impart our giftedness to the world. You see, nourishing your spirit fosters an internal environment that sets you up to give freely and fully. Once you begin mothering from a feeling of internal fullness, you change the atmosphere in your home and family, as well as the way in which you function in the world. Your relationship with your children is enriched as you experience a feeling of profound connection with them. This is why nourishing your spirit through self-care - or inner-care - is the single most effective practice you can engage in.

What It Means to Thrive

We all know people who have felt lonely and longed for a relationship, yet when they find that relationship they discover they are still lonely. Then, too, there are those who work their way up into high-powered careers, but who once there find they are burned out. Even women who are considered exceedingly beautiful, and perhaps in great shape, are frequently unhappy with and even highly critical of their bodies.

Our culture confuses our essential nature with the things we *do*. It touts the idea that we can receive value from doing. The consequence is that much of society is driven to achieve. In other words, because we mistakenly believe ourselves to be inadequate, lacking in some way, we tend to think we need to overcompensate by doing. Perhaps we work hard and long. But no matter how hard or how long we work, we will never "do" our way into worthiness.

The outer trappings of career, money, relationship and family, beauty and health, don't in and of themselves bring fulfillment. This is because to truly thrive is an *internal* experience.

It may come as a surprise, but my counseling experience tells me that children don't really care how much money we make or how large our house is. They simply want to feel connected to us. They long to feel seen and heard by us. This is what, when we were children, we too longed for.

Thriving is different from acquiring things—whether material possessions, prestige, or relationships. To thrive is to experience a state of well-being that arises right in the middle of the busy and often exhausting lives we lead as mothers.

To live a life in which we are thriving and can therefore truly serve others, especially our children, requires us to connect with our inherent *being*. This is how we correct our inaccurate, but highly convincing thinking that we are in some way lacking, broken, or damaged.

Once you accept yourself exactly as you are right now, you will know no scarcity, no lack, no feeling of victimhood. No matter what may have happened to you in your past or what you think about your life right now, your *intrinsic* value can *never be diminished*. In fact, nothing you do can either add value to your being or take away from it. So even if you think of yourself as "inadequate," your thoughts can't make it so.

The experience of fulfillment is something quite distinct from your circumstances and entirely separate from whatever you may or may not do or achieve in life.

Instead of seeking fulfillment externally—such as through our children—we are asked to explore our *inherent* being from the inside out. We cease allowing our external circumstances to define our identity—things like our children's grades, the school they attend, awards they win, achievements they accomplish. The payoff of knowing our own unalloyed self is exponential.

Once you realize this, even the smallest, simplest act of self-care will begin to reconnect you with your true nature, which is whole and abundant, overflowing with value and worth. You'll find yourself treasuring yourself, which is the experience of fulfillment.

The reason self-care shifts our experience of motherhood from one of lack, whereby we feel run ragged, to fulfillment is that we are simply embracing *what's already true of us,* which is that at our center we have all the love, joy, peace, and every other value we could ever need. Although this deeper aspect of ourselves may feel elusive to us, the practice of nourishing our spirit reconnects us with this powerful sense of self that's our essential being.

My client Laura relates how this happened for her:

My sense of self-esteem—and therefore my mothering experience—was rooted in my accomplishments. Wanting to be a good mother, I did so much for my children. Yet over and over, I felt as if I was failing miserably. I realized I didn't have a sense of myself based on who I am inside. It was during a session with you—I remember it vividly. I can hear you asking, "What would it be like for you to value yourself, to treasure yourself?"

On the other end of the phone, my face was clenching and my eyebrows were furrowed. I didn't know what you were talking about! I think I even asked, "What do you mean?"

Your reply was for me to consider myself to the same degree I took in caring for my children and everyone and everything around me. I really liked the concept of treasuring myself. I could relate somehow because I treasured my children.

I began to experiment with what it would look like to treasure myself. I became aware of how I felt in different situations with my children. My intuition became my guide. If something didn't feel right, I paused and contemplated it rather than reacting and then acting it out with my children. What wasn't feeling right? It became apparent that I had built a family life with my children where I felt disregarded. I was disregarding myself.

I learned that the more I cared for myself, the closer my relationship became with each of my three children. I learned to say "no" to things my children or others ask me to do if they will be done with resentment, a sense of "I should do this," or if my "being" will be affected by taking it on. Valuing myself means considering myself in the equation and asking for what I need instead of staying invisible in the background. It means to slow down and really check in with myself before committing.

Learning to value myself is a process that has brought me calm, happiness, and a letting go of feeling like I'm "nothing." I learned that relief from the feeling of being invisible doesn't come when my children treat me a certain way. Rather, it began to shift when I perceived myself differently and taught those around me what I saw. I found out that I am lovable, and that's priceless. I learned I'm worthy of my own time and attention.

Now I treasure this lovable me and all those around me, especially my children.

When we first treasure ourselves, we begin to speak more kindly to our children, have more empathy for their feelings, and experience a deeper connection with them—or perhaps reestablish a connection that's been all but absent.

In addition to treasuring ourselves, we want our daughters and sons to treasure themselves. How does this come about? As we treasure ourselves, our very presence will teach them to treasure themselves.

Society isn't going to treasure us, though it may well lavish on us adulation as long as we are "accomplishing" in the way it expects of us. Corporate America isn't going to acknowledge our importance as an individual in our own right. Treasuring ourselves as mothers is something entirely different from the kinds of things society values, such as celebrity and overachievement.

Treasuring ourselves comes simply from within, from delighting in our *being*. This is particularly important for mothers. If there's a group of people on the planet who need the ability to treasure ourselves and experience a sense of well-being in the midst of everything going on around us, it's mothers.

You Are a Person of Inestimable Value

So how do we become acquainted with our essential being, with its inherent sense of worth?

When we first look into a child's eyes, we can actually see their being, and how they love simply being who they are. Because children wear no mask and engage in no pretense, we get to see right to their essence, by which I mean their most natural state. When we do so, we recognize intuitively that children are valuable simply because they *are*.

Infants haven't *done* anything, accomplished anything, to make themselves worthy. Rather, they are worthy because of their very *being*. There will be lots of "doing" in their lifetime, and they may accomplish plenty. However, neither their accomplishments, no matter how great, nor the accolades that may go along with these accomplishments can add to their essential value. There will also be shortcomings and missteps, though none of these will detract from their inherent worth, since nothing can tarnish a person's fundamental nature.

You may have lost touch with your essential worth, as a result of which you imagine your achievements are what give you your value. Or perhaps you think the ways in which you've stumbled, maybe even on a grand scale at times, detract from who you are. But none of this affects your naturally worthy state. None of it detracts from the magnificent being you are beneath your achievements or your blunders.

Are you beginning to get the picture? You are worthy just because you *are*.

As you become reacquainted with your inborn sense of worth, you'll begin to experience your original essence shining through all of your mistakes, growth, learning, and successes. You'll no longer measure your worth according to your behavior, but instead have the ability to witness your original nature—the same nature parents see in children the moment they meet. When this happens, you can't help but treasure yourself.

Now is the time for each of us to recapture our own original state of being. At this moment in history, both individually and collectively, we have an opportunity to turn the cultural message of scarcity on its head. As we value our "being" first and foremost, recognizing ourselves as someone of worth rather than someone in whom there's lack, the things we accomplish in life will come about without "efforting"—that is, without any need to overcompensate.

Anything we do that's rooted in our intrinsic worth constitutes a joyful returning of the gifts already given to us by life itself. Rather than a feeling of having achieved something through a long and difficult struggle, doing what springs from knowing our value has an abundantly fulfilling element to it. This is the glory of our true being.

If we are to reconnect with our intrinsic worth, and hence with our internal abundance, care of our spirit is the most helpful practice we can engage in. When we nourish our essence, we wake up places within us that have long been asleep. By caring for our spirit, we demonstrate to ourselves that we are lavishly supported and provided for.

It Starts with a Vision

Spiritual teacher Michael Bernard Beckwith says that a true mother is someone who holds the highest vision of her child. We can hold that vision best when we first learn to hold the highest vision of ourselves as mothers. How many of us have even thought about holding a high vision of *ourselves* as mothers?

There's a cultural phenomenon many mothers I work with seem to experience that I call "the good mother syndrome." We seek to be good mothers without really defining what this actually means to us as mothers. Consequently, being a good mother becomes about trying to attain some imagined "perfect" mother status, moving us away from our inner wisdom, being, and spiritual connection, and catapulting us into the external world of comparisons, competition, activities and accomplishments.

One of the reasons mothers slip into this way of mothering so easily is because we aren't taught to take the time to set intentions and create a vision for ourselves as mothers from the inside-out. One day we are a woman, the next day we are a mother and because we can't possibly imagine what the experience of motherhood will entail, and rarely does anyone really share with us the daunting aspects of motherhood, mothers typically create a fantasy, rather than an actual vision of motherhood.

Perhaps you've heard the proverb, "Without vision, the people perish." Says Michael Bernard Beckwith, "The pain pushes until the vision pulls." The pain of motherhood will push us, until we create a higher vision for ourselves as women and mothers.

One of the most liberating things you can do for yourself as a mother is to release the fantasy of being a good mother and instead seek to become a fulfilled mother. Learning to hold a high vision of myself as a woman and mother has transformed my relationship within myself, my husband and my son. It's not a stretch to say that contemplating, journaling and holding the highest vision of *yourself* as a mother will transform your life. You'll find yourself naturally seeing the best in your children when you hold a high vision of yourself.

I love taking mothers through a process of contemplating the qualities of motherhood they seek to embody. The wisdom that comes through mothers is astounding to me.

For instance, I recently led my client Sherry, mother of two boys ages two and six, through this process when she came to me overwhelmed, burned out, and feeling like anything but the "good mother" she sought to be. I guided her as, with her eyes closed, she delved into the qualities of motherhood that were meaningful to her.

She began describing to me how her pregnancies were the best times of motherhood, since being pregnant gave her the "permission" she needed to care for herself. After all, her babies were inside her. She ate well, worked out, got plenty of rest, and immersed herself in all things inspirational. However, after Aidan was born, all bets were off. She was so focused on caring for Aidan that self-care fell away without her even noticing. Consequently, those first few years were torture for Sherry. She was sleep deprived, irritable, and took it all out on Aidan and her husband Joe.

When Sherry again became pregnant, since she was carrying Charlie and his health depended upon her health, she once more began caring for herself. "When I look back, I don't even know how I did it so easily," she related. "Aidan was three-years-old and self-care wasn't even an issue. I just knew I wanted to be at my best for Charlie..."

Sherry's voice trailed off as she had an epiphany. "Not only did I take the time to eat well, work out, and rest, but I absolutely immersed myself in inspirational books and activities—not just for myself, but also for Aidan. That time was by far my best and most connected time with him. We took hikes together and spent lots of hours at the park lost in time, picking wildflowers, or looking for four-leaf clovers, lizards, and other creatures. We lay in bed together at night and I'd tell him stories about his little brother coming to us. It was a magical time for Aidan, and me as well."

Realizing that giving herself permission to nourish her spirit when pregnant with Charlie created a close connection with Aidan, so that he benefitted from her self-care, Sherry was able to create a vision for herself as a mother that came from her own inner wisdom. It was a matter of knowing what was important to *her*, rather than society's idea of what a good mother looks like.

Lower Your Motherhood Bar

Another client, Penny, with two young children, Abby age six and Erica age four, stumbled upon her vision of motherhood after being sick for over a week. She explained,

It was getting sick last year that first gave me permission to take care of myself. The first few days, I tried to power through the flu, caring for my girls, thinking that if I ignored the fact I was sick, it would go away.

You suggested I "lower the bar" on my own expectations of myself. So, somewhere around day three, I ordered pizza for dinner for the kids. By day four, Abby was making a peanut butter and jelly sandwich for Erica for breakfast. There was such a marked difference between the mother trying to power through the flu and the surrendered mother on the couch—not so much in the external activities, but in my state of being. I actually felt better as my flu got worse. My girls were happier. They had the time of their life making those sandwiches. All on their own, they cleaned up the kitchen, played nurse, and made me get well cards. We actually had a good time despite the fact I was feeling miserable. Taking care of myself brought out the best in my girls, something I would never have expected.

I liked who I was as a mother during that time and I wanted to keep her around. I felt more relaxed within myself and more connected with my girls. It sounds dramatic to say this, but that week with the flu changed my life. Lowering the bar on my own self-inflicted expectations allowed a vision of the mother I truly am to come flooding into me.

Penny learned that taking care of herself *is* being a good mother.

I find a longing within mothers to reconnect with the intimate bond they initially experienced with their children. When we look deeper, we discover that their real desire is to experience this connection within *themselves*. I know this was the case for me after having my son.

There is a spiritual energy that's an untapped power within mothers—one that, once we tap into it, empowers us from the inside out and can change everything about our life as a mother.

3

Self-Care Isn't for the Faint of Heart

What do I mean when I speak of "self-care?" Well, for a start, self-care *isn't* one more thing to add to your to-do list.

Let me also state upfront that self-care shouldn't be equated with self-pampering or self-indulgence—although, paradoxically, it includes both, and sometimes it's self-pampering that leads us into the even richer experience that self-care can bring.

Self-care, or inner-care as I call it, is the practice of nurturing ourselves on the physical, mental, emotional, and spiritual levels in order that we may experience an ecstatic sense of well-being, vitality, and fulfillment. It's the bridge to living an expansive, enlightened life, especially where our children are concerned.

Self-care provides for our innermost self that which we did not receive when we ourselves were young. This inner-care is the way that we, as mothers now, meet our own unmet needs. When we attempt to parent our children with unmet needs of our own, we will unconsciously look to them to meet our needs. We'll be continually triggered when they don't in fact meet our needs - which, of course, they are not here to do. We won't have the bandwidth to be fully present, available and engaged to meet theirs.

Self-care reminds us we are connected to something greater than our individual and family life, an infinite, inexhaustible wellspring of good that's always available to us if we but partake of it. This inner spring is available to bring fresh life to every area of our existence, and in particular our role as a mother. In my counseling practice, I find that mothers yearn to relate to their children from this awakened state of being.

Spirituality isn't different from our humanity—isn't, in fact, in any way separate from it. Spirituality is *an awakened way of being human.* Our spirituality enhances our humanity by infusing it with qualities like awe, gratitude, love, contentment, patience, peace, joy, and meaning. It's a way of living that emanates from and encompasses the whole of ourselves.

Tapping into our spirituality is at the heart of self-care.

The Quality of Your Life

"The entire notion of self-care is foreign to me," my client Brianna began. "When you first introduced this idea to me, I remember wondering, 'What in the world does that mean—self-care?'"

Brianna went on to explain:

My life changed dramatically with the birth of my daughter, Gabby. I was focused on providing for her. My career success reflected my desire to create a life filled with opportunities for fun, learning, travel, culture, and all the happiness that life has to offer. We enjoyed the "good life" and I was the primary provider.

I recently lost my husband and, within a short time, my career opportunities also evaporated. Through it all, it never occurred to me to take care of myself. And so I didn't—not at all.

I tried to continue to be a good mother, a good friend, a good employee, but without the "spark" that inspires—the "what for"--I lost my way. Depression became my reality. Joy was a joke. I even considered suicide. The sad truth is that if I couldn't "check out" because of Gabby, then I would "numb out" with food, alcohol, shopping, and staying busy.

I was busy, very busy. I went to appointments, meetings, and planning sessions. Where I didn't always go was to the gym, the dance class, the doctor, weight watchers, or support groups for taking care of my physical self, much less my emotional and spiritual self.

In all of this, I was missing *me*.

Today, as I set out to find myself, I'm taking baby steps to reconnect with this long-lost self. I'm learning to take care of myself and discovering that it's worth my time and attention—that it's saving my life.

I've begun to slow down. I'm seeking to live in a way that honors and takes care of my whole self. I've begun sharing with my closest mother friends and finding they feel the same way. Even these more meaningful conversations seem nourishing like a warm glass of milk. We all seem to be searching for something deeper, a sense of purpose and meaning. We want to make a valuable contribution to life. We want to know that our lives are important, that we matter. I know this is what I want.

I'm no longer running on empty. I'm on my way to "full." I feel a spark I haven't felt in a long while. Something's alive within me, and I'm beginning to imagine the quality of life that's actually possible for me. I don't want to live my life without this anymore. More than anything else, I'm realizing that taking even the smallest of steps toward caring for myself changes entirely the way I feel about myself, and Gabby feels this too.

Brianna's experience speaks for so many clients I see who seek something beyond what their current experience of life provides for them, especially where raising children is concerned.

I often hear it said that we are "spiritual beings having a human experience." Through both personal experience and my many years of counseling others, I have found that what we really seem to be seeking is to have our human life infused with the spiritual qualities of connection, love, joy, peace, inspiration, abundance, creativity, patience, and purpose. We want our life to be bathed in these qualities. Especially as mothers, so much continually reminds us of just how "human" we are. So while I understand what people mean when they speak of us as spiritual beings having a human experience, I prefer to say we are spiritual beings seeking a *spiritual* experience of what it means to be on this earth raising our children.

I work with clients who have worked so hard to enroll their children in the best schools and activities. Often when they have everything they have dreamed of, they discover that the things they worked so diligently to acquire are actually quite empty in and of themselves. They don't result in the kind of relationship they yearn for with their children.

It's at this point that mothers sometimes discover that what they have actually been seeking all along is a *quality* of life with their children—a relationship with them that they mistakenly thought the material realm would provide. The great news is that it's not a case of either-or. Rather, it's when our life is characterized by spiritual qualities that the material world becomes meaningful. These qualities enrich our experience of the very things we've sought as ends in themselves, most importantly our connection to and relationship with our children.

Inner-care consciously connects us with our spirit, which is an individual manifestation of the infinite spirit of life itself. Inner-care allows us to experience ourselves as whole instead of broken or damaged.

Just like electricity, the infinite generosity of the universe is always available, since it's the ground of our own being. But we need to be plugged in before it can be activated in our life, and this happens through awareness. Inner-care is a way of plugging ourselves in.

Our children feel whether we are connected or disconnected. Simply walking into the room when we are connected invites them into a safe haven. What a different childhood we provide for our children when we are connected. When we are plugged in, our children light up.

From Simply Surviving to Powerfully Thriving

Henry David Thoreau was so insightful when he commented that most people live lives of "quiet desperation." I certainly find this with our journey as mothers. What do such lives look like? All too often they consist of the very things we've been told should be our dream—the career, the 2.5 children, and the house with the white picket fence, not to mention doing the countless things in a day that we are told makes us a good mother.

Whereas the endless tasks that come with motherhood involve us in the material aspects of our existence, inner-care allows us to access the invisible, inexhaustible wisdom that's always available to fuel our life when we are consciously connected to it.

Take for example my client Laila. With only one child, there was great pressure on her from both her family and her husband's to have more children. Having grown up to believe that not to provide a sibling for her daughter would prove to be detrimental to her little girl and therefore be selfish on her part as a mother, Laila herself experienced tremendous conflict over the issue.

But Laila also heard a deeper call than the voice of family and social pressure—the call of her own wisdom. Something inside her that she could only describe as an "inner knowing" told her that her family was complete. Despite the immense conflict this triggered, she found the courage to follow her own guidance rather than succumb to the pressure of family and society. She's at peace within herself. She has created the family she was meant to create and thriving as the mother she is meant to be.

When our children see us living a life that's meaningful and fulfilled, it gives them permission to pursue their own unique experience of fulfillment. When it comes to raising children, nothing is more contagious than a mother who is living her life full-on. Nothing is more inspiring than an evident sense of fulfillment.

4

The Martyred Mother

Women, particularly mothers, have been inducted into a long lineage of martyrdom, both within our individual families and culturally as a whole.

A martyr is an individual who endures great suffering on behalf of a belief or cause. We mothers endure great suffering when we care for our children to the *exclusion* of ourselves, thinking we're doing something *for* them. But, is this working for us? And to what end?

Depriving ourselves is a leftover of the austere, rigid life of the Puritan era. In modern times, the word "Puritan" is often used to mean "against pleasure." When we buy into the outdated, Puritan mindset of lack and limitation, it leads us to abandon ourselves, to put ourselves last, and to, in a very real sense, martyr ourselves.

On the other hand, our culture today entices us to overindulge in the external, trying to convince us that outer riches and pleasure can feed our deep inner hunger for real soul satisfaction and a connection to something greater than what outer life can provide us.

With such an approach to life, we either create deprivation or indulgence instead of true abundance. In contrast, when we have the courage to care for ourselves, we create a sense of fulfillment —and joy—from the inside out that overrides the restrictive rules and regulations that we have bought into for so long.

As recently as the 1950s, most mothers were full-time homemakers with extended family living nearby to assist whenever help was needed. When women and mothers entered the workplace, they tended to adopt the patriarchal model that had long been the mode of the world of business. They did so because this was their doorway in. However, entering a patriarchal system and using masculine energy has left not only women but the workplace itself in a severely imbalanced and impoverished state. A great many mothers in the workplace find themselves depleted of energy, exhausted, and in no small number of cases completely burned out as a result of operating in this predominantly masculine mode.

Working mothers, women—and, dare I say, men also—yearn for a work life that has meaning. Many of my "mom" clients are starting their own businesses as a way of finding meaning, and an entirely new segment of the parenting population are referred to as "mompreneurs." However, the temptation—and, from my experience, the tendency in many cases—is to run these businesses in the masculine mode. Even many stay-at-home mothers who don't start businesses also use their masculine energy more than their innate feminine energy.

Instead of falling into the old patterns, this is the time for women, and mothers especially, to trust our feminine—and ultimately, spiritual—energy to source our life and relationships with our children, which will bring forth businesses and a family life that are grounded in "being" rather than "doing," abundance, rather than lack, and therefore flourish.

Wearing the Pants

Thinking she was doing a good thing for her family, Teresa shared with me that for thirteen years she had been the one who "wore the pants in the family.» It was a role she took on because she had a precise picture of how she wanted to raise her two girls. She felt her husband Jim was pretty easygoing and wouldn't mind at all.

It turned out this wasn't quite the case. "The fact is, it was at a high price," Teresa confided. As she explained:

Jim has expressed that he feels I tend to talk *at* him. The dynamic of our relationship is that I'm in charge—"Teresa calls the shots," as he puts it—and he's my subordinate. This has strained our relationship, and the girls notice it. They see how he's more easygoing and detached, and I'm more rigid and controlling. They sense we aren't an equal team. They tend to gravitate toward him, such as hanging out with him more often.

I am working on trying to let Jim take the lead, not micromanaging how he is with the girls, lightening up a bit. It has been hard, as he makes different choices than I would around food, media, bedtime, homework, and routines in general. Whenever I'm less controlling about these things, I notice how my relationship with my husband and daughters feels lighter, more spacious. They also reach for me more often. Whereas when I control their choices, there's a lessening of intimacy, more distance than closeness, as they subtly retreat.

I have been far too hands-on and strict with my oldest daughter, Cindy, particularly over things like food choices. Because I haven't given her some freedom around this, she has rebelled to an extreme. She now wants to eat solely junk food. I know that all kids rebel to some extent, and trying different things is part of growing up and eventually becoming independent. But this is outright rejection of my restrictive ways, not about her rightful developmental journey. Deep down, I realize that were I more balanced about things, my daughter would probably have had no need to go to such an extreme. Today, the question I'm more and more asking myself is, "Do I want to be in control, or do I want to be close to my family?"

I'm learning to slow down, be less rigid with myself and take the time to take care of me. When I do, I come to the relationship with Jim and my girls with patience and the ability to talk through and process issues in our life, rather than talk at them. More importantly, I have a reserve of energy within myself, so that when I feel the urge to control come, I am able to resist the temptation to act out upon it.

For instance, yesterday, Jim took the girls out for dinner. In the past, I'd have made sure to grill him on what he should and shouldn't allow the girls to order and try to control the amount of sugar and desserts they'd have. I'd remind the girls of the same thing before they left the house. Yesterday, I genuinely wanted them to have a good time and was so relaxed within myself when they left. I went for a run and when they returned and told me about their time together, I was listening with sincere interest rather than fishing for clues about what they ate. They laughed and joked about how they all ordered two desserts each, trying to get a reaction out of me! Turns out, they chose to order one dessert for the table and felt great about their choice.

I feel so proud that I'd gone for a run myself. My entire way of being is different when I'm full. I like being around me more!

As we become aware of how we tend to exist within an outdated, ineffective paradigm that doesn't nurture our soul, we can consciously choose a new practice of self-care, valuing ourselves, and taking personal responsibility for our life and choices. In this way we won't recreate in our children and thereby pass down to future generations a victim mentality, poisoning them with the toxic energy of the martyr.

I like to say that martyrdom is so last century! Each of us is here to experience fulfillment, and an important aspect of doing this is to reclaim our most powerful assets as mothers, which consist of our *feminine* and ultimately, spiritual qualities of being.

There's a hunger within mothers to contribute our ability to connect and create deep bonds of intimacy, forming strong relationships, all of which bring meaning into our families and the workplace. For this hunger to be satisfied, we must come to know ourselves to be more than enough, whole and abundant, lacking nothing.

Corporate America, society in general, or even our significant other if we have one may not acknowledge us yet, but we can value our qualities ourselves, as well as valuing them in each other as women and mothers.

By coming together, our voice will be authentically amplified without having to succumb to a more masculine way of being.

Collectively, the natural giftedness of the feminine and the qualities of the mother such as intimacy and connection, the ability to process and relate, nourishing and nurturing, mother's intuition and spiritual power can change the world. All it awaits is for us to occupy our rightful place.

From Depriving to Thriving

We are taught to believe that sacrifice is noble—that the more we do at our own expense, the more selfless we appear. So we give and give of ourselves. Disconnected from our true nature, since we haven't nurtured it, we try to "do" ourselves into "being" enough. Before long we feel depleted. This is all based on a belief in lack and creates anxiety, both individual and cultural.

We're talking about the way we've been indoctrinated with the idea that taking care of ourselves is selfish and that to put ourselves first would be practically a sin.

We are all in agreement that we want to take good care of our children. However, we can't give away what we don't have. For example, I can't give you a $100 bill if I don't have one to give. Well, it's no different with taking care of our children. This is why it's so important we have a full tank.

Inner-care is the most effective cure for any tendency we may have to martyr ourselves because self-care gradually shifts us into a consciousness of abundance. Self-care is the best medicine for society's message that the more we do, the more worthy we are.

Filling Your *Own* Tank

The only enduring sense of identity is that which comes from our own center as we hear the call of our soul and have the courage to follow it.

After becoming a mother, my client Alice became less and less enchanted with living in the city and more and more committed to finding a different quality of life for her family. She envisioned raising her children in a small town, a place where they could ride their bikes to school, where there was plenty of clean air, and where they could enjoy a slower pace than she felt she could provide in the city.

When Alice first conceived of this, it seemed an impossibility because her husband was a playwright and the city seemed like the place he needed to be for his work. After countless conversations between the two of them and multiple meetings with his agents, her husband agreed to move their family upstate and continue his career long-distance. They found a simple but beautiful property and the move seemed ideal. They loved the more easygoing lifestyle, and the natural surroundings nourished them all. Alice's husband wrote from home, commuting to the city every few months for meetings.

Although Alice had created the kind of outer life she had envisioned for her family, she often found herself plagued by an emptiness in the pit of her stomach. She tried to ignore this gnawing void, feeling she was somewhat of a spoiled brat. What right did she have to complain? After all, her husband had relocated for her and she was truly grateful. Nevertheless, she found herself increasingly criticizing her husband for the smallest of things. It seemed like every day brought more and more bickering, to the point that the situation became tense.

Alice judged herself harshly for her behavior. Even though she was sincerely seeking a close marriage and happy family life, she was unable to shake the empty feeling that was eating away at her, which caused her to take her unhappiness out on her husband.

Because her husband was working so hard to support them, Alice felt guilty about spending money on herself. She focused on providing her children with nutritious food—although it was challenging for her to even justify buying the organic foods she preferred because of the extra cost. Little by little though, as a practice of self-care, she purchased more and more of them.

Because buying organic was so much more expensive, she made sure to prepare the food with great love, looking up recipes and experimenting with different ways of turning a regular dinner into something really special for her family. She loved the entire preparation process, the flavor of the food, the way it made her feel, and the deep gratitude she felt that she was able to provide for her family in a way that was true to her innermost being.

Alice began talking with other mothers about organic foods, nutrition, and recipes. She encouraged a friend who was quite the organic chef to start a group for mothers to get together once a week to exchange and experiment with different recipes. These evenings became the highlight of her week.

Over time, Alice's love of organic foods claimed a more prominent place in her life. When a mother in the group told her about a six-week organic cooking class that takes place in France every summer, Alice knew in her heart that she had to go. During the course of the next year she saved every penny she could.

The time came when, despite conflicting feelings about leaving her husband to care for their two children while she was out of the country, Alice took the leap, going on a trip that was to change her life. She returned from France dedicated to becoming a personal chef. Now, five years later, she is inwardly fulfilled with a beautiful business of her own that she loves.

Alice shared with me how it was when she finally gave herself permission to take care of herself that she was able to access the contentment she had been lacking in her life. Of course! She had identified and answered the call of her soul.

Research shows that those with vitality, who feel most alive, are the *first* to contribute to the needs of others. The greater our sense of well-being, the more energy we have, and the more likely we are to serve those around us. We feel impelled not only to make *our* world a better place, but to make *the* world a better place.

5

Guilt—the Martyr's Cousin

Mothers feel guilty when we take care of ourselves. Mothers feel guilty when we *don't* take care of ourselves. Rarely does a day go by that one of my clients doesn't tell me how guilty she feels.

We experience feelings of guilt when we believe we're doing something wrong. Most of the time, we've inherited these beliefs of what's right and wrong from our families and culture without ever stopping to consider whether these beliefs are even working in our lives. These limiting beliefs are born of lack and leave us in a double bind, damned if we take care of ourselves and damned if we don't.

Beneath the belief that we are *doing* something wrong is the belief that who we *are* is wrong somehow, that our being is flawed in some way. So we create "to do" lists that we somehow imagine will make us "enough." We think that our "doing" can somehow make up for our perceived inadequacy. We tell ourselves that if we overcompensate for our inadequate *being* by *doing* enough, we'll finally rid ourselves of the distressing voice within us that erroneously, but intensely, whispers that who we *are* is flawed, even shameful.

Of course, we can never do enough to silence this voice, since it isn't our true voice but is a learned one from society that drowns out our own voice.

Discovering Your Intrinsic Innocence

In the West, the majority of us have been taught about original sin, which has defined so many of us as essentially flawed. But how many of us have gone deeper than this and discovered our *original innocence?*

Think back to the moment you looked into your newborn's eyes. We don't look into the eyes of a newborn and see original sin. We see an incredible innocence.

In the East, the idea of original sin isn't part of the culture. Rather than feeling there's something wrong with them, people who embrace Eastern philosophies tend to think of themselves in terms of how they appear to others—whether they are a person of honor, respected by their family and society, or whether they bring shame on the family.

If you look closely at both the Eastern and Western ideas of our humanity, we are all concerned about—and I might even say deeply worried about—how we are performing, whether in our own eyes or in the eyes of others. In both East and West, it comes down to whether we understand ourselves in terms of our *being* or in terms of our *doing*.

Our inherent nature is good—the very image and likeness of God—and can't be compromised. It's only how we've been taught to see ourselves that's off target. Our inherent nature is a *God-given guiltlessness!*

Natalie, mother to a six-month-old, Penelope, learned of her own guiltlessness. As parents of an infant, both Natalie and her husband were sleep deprived. Much as Natalie tried to give herself permission to rest when her daughter was napping, she couldn't stop her mind from rattling off the list of things she ought to be doing while her child slept.

Before Penelope was born, Natalie and her husband worked full-time to make ends meet. Natalie assumed she would go back to work after her maternity leave came to an end. But with Penelope in her life, she realized she didn't want to go back to work; she wanted to stay home, at least a little while longer. Her husband agreed to become the sole financial provider for their family.

On top of the endless list of things that needed tending to while her daughter napped, Natalie felt guilty at the thought of lying down, then having her husband come home to a messy house or dirty dishes in the sink. After all, he was gone all day, allowing her to be home with Penelope.

As a way of showing her gratitude to her husband for the precious time she was able to spend with Penelope, she decided to take on all the night feedings. She also committed herself to making sure the house was clean and the dishes done when her husband arrived home each evening. Natalie and her husband found themselves increasingly exhausted, and this was taking a heavy toll on their relationship.

As a counselor, I'm acutely aware of how common this scenario is in today's families. With my encouragement, Natalie began taking baby steps toward self-care. Even in the midst of her feelings of guilt, she would lie down on her bed and put on some music as Penelope napped. Then she'd get up and do chores. She also kept music playing as she worked.

Natalie began enjoying a rich connection with her daughter in the afternoons that she hadn't really experienced before. Taking a nap with her daughter provided her with more than a physical rest in the middle of the day. The ritual of lying down together allowed her to turn away from her world and turn toward the world that lay within her—a world that restores and nourishes our soul. With Natalie's soul restored, her afternoons were transformed into a time of great intimacy with her daughter that she treasured beyond measure.

On one particular occasion when she had given herself permission to nap with Penelope, Natalie's husband returned home after work to find a pile of laundry on the dining room table and his wife folding it. As she asked about his day, her husband naturally began to fold the laundry with her as they chatted. There they were, Natalie utterly relaxed with Penelope in a sling held close to her body, music playing in the background, connecting over their day while performing a chore together. Such a simple scene. Experiencing a profound feeling of bliss, Natalie was in heaven.

It was in this situation that a lightbulb went off in Natalie's head. All the guilt she had been carrying was a burden *she* had placed on *herself*. She had internalized the voice of her own mother, layering on it the messages of society, thereby drowning out her own true voice—the voice that told her taking a nap at times would be so valuable.

Deep down, Natalie knew that this phase of her daughter's infancy would be gone in the blink of an eye. She became aware of a deep yearning within her to truly experience this rich time before it slipped through her fingertips.

For Natalie this was a moment of authentic acknowledgment of herself, an appreciation of her ability to turn away from all those messages of society that had stopped her doing the very things that, now that she could see clearly, she realized had obviously been needed all along. Turning away from messages of lack allowed her to turn toward messages of abundance, with more than enough for everyone to have their needs met.

What if, instead of feeling guilty, we were to see our desire to care for ourselves as an innocent intention to better serve both ourselves and our children?

Once you see your intention to care for yourself as *innocent*, you will never feel guilty again.

What if we were to trust our inner authority - over any cultural authority - understanding that the best way for us to truly care for our children is to make sure we are healthy in body, mind, and spirit?

What if we were to believe in our natural state of abundance—that who we are is already enough, and that there is more than enough for everyone to have their needs met?

I do believe that we know, deep within us, that the better we care for ourselves, the *better* we'll care of our children. This is the state of guiltlessness.

Guilt-free Giving

Have you ever felt uncomfortable with all those messages family and society give us about what we should or shouldn't be doing—messages that create so much of the guilt we feel? If you've felt a measure of discomfort, have you thought about where that discomfort comes from?

As we discussed a little while ago, we feel guilty because we believe we're doing something wrong when we take care of ourselves. But look deeper. The real reason these messages don't feel good is that they rub up against our true nature, for which it's natural to give. We are all wired to give, and our wisdom tells us that beliefs commanding us to deny giving to ourselves or others are unnecessary. We're all givers by nature.

Authentic giving comes from an overflow of feeling great. When we care for our true nature, our inner-most Self, we find that our spontaneous desire to give that was there all along, comes shining through. Self-caring creates an inner overflow that transforms guilt-ridden "doing," that's motivated by "have to's," to a joyful "being" in which we happily "get to" do things for others. We're resentful when we're trying to give from an empty tank. We're grateful to give when it comes from an overflow.

When we feel guilty as a result of measuring ourselves against society's standards, including all those internalized voices we mistake for our own, the answer is to turn within and connect with our inherent wisdom, our deepest mother's intuition, which understands precisely what we need in any situation.

Deep within, we know we aren't meant to take care of everyone else at our own expense. We also know we aren't about to take care of ourselves at the expense of neglecting our children. We no longer need to buy into the either-or mentality of lack, which tells us that to take care of ourselves means someone else will be deprived. Quite the reverse, a consciousness of abundance loves to give. When we connect with our inner wisdom and allow it to speak more powerfully than the voices of society, whether these are external voices or ones we have internalized, we will empower ourselves, our children, our families, society, and the world.

I once heard someone put a twist on the "grass is greener" axiom. Said this individual, "The grass is always greener *where you water it*." This reworked axiom is one mothers need to hear, since our spirits shrivel up from lack of being watered. When we don't take the time to water our garden, it shrivels up. When we take the time to water our garden, it flourishes.

You Can Be Free of Guilt's Grip

Stephanie shared with me her journey of learning to live free of guilt. Expressing her desire "to be the best mother I can be, the best human being I can be," Stephanie began with how, as mothers, our parenting reflects the way we are feeling on the inside at any given moment. She explained:

I feel as though, early in my parenting, I was operating from a place of expectations, some of them originating in myself and others from society. These revolved around comparing, competing, and a feeling of lack. As mothers, a lot's expected of us. We tend to measure our worth by how much we are doing and giving, and how this will be seen through the eyes of others, not just our own. Along with other mothers, I frequently found myself comparing and judging (whether silently or to others), competing (often trying to outdo others in order to feel good about myself), and operating from a perfectionism driven by my sense of lack and need to compensate. There was a lot of pressure, both internal and external.

This type of environment was constricting and not at all supportive of me when it comes to tapping into the wealth that lies within. I was giving my power away by allowing external circumstances, opinions, and judgments to determine how I felt about myself. Life became a chore, an obligation, exhausting instead of satisfying. I felt neither nourished nor whole. Nor was I "present" in my life, but was instead operating from my overactive mind rather than my center, my heart, my spirit. In a nutshell, I was experiencing neither inner peace nor contentment.

Everything shifted for me when I started to care for myself. I decided I was going to take some time to nourish my heart, setting up the conditions in my life that would allow me to feel happy, whole, content, and at peace. I wasn't sure how I'd do this. Then I discovered yoga. This became a time just for me—a retreat of sorts, where I could afford to let my mind become quiet. In due course I began to feel more balanced, along with a natural sense of ease, a lightness, and an inner spaciousness. It was as if I at last had breathing room.

As a married woman and a mother, I was able to stay in my center, the heart, and deeply listen to my children and my spouse. They felt more seen and heard. In fact, they felt honored and appreciated—all because I was at last giving these things to myself.

Finding myself becoming more present, the need for lots of activity slowed, both for myself and for them. As I gave myself the gift of time and really listened to what was arising inside me, my connection with my kids and husband deepened. Deepening myself deepened my relationship with them.

I began to teach yoga a few days a week and took a three-week trip to India. There's great wisdom in the saying, "Follow your bliss." As we touch our bliss, it allows others to remember what they already intuit deep down about their own need to access their bliss.

When I'm a mother operating from my mind, I'm reactive, scattered, busy, and not very present. When I'm a mother of the heart, I'm centered, spacious, calm, present, and at peace. Tapping into my inner wealth, I feel my life to be abundant. I also feel free.

The greatest gift I can give myself and my family is to grow my ability to remain in my center, the still point, the place of pure peace and presence, which is something I've discovered is available to me always. But it takes practice to remain there.

Through self-care, I get out of my head and into my heart. It's a discipline that serves me and all those in my life. For me home is where the heart is. I should add that self-care looks a bit different for each person, but what matters is that we are learning to be at home in ourselves. Coming home to myself, again and again, is my spiritual practice.

What if I told you that guilt and martyrdom are detrimental to your child's healthy sense of self, and that taking care of yourself first is beneficial to them? Caring for yourself—your life, your spirit—awakens your natural state of abundance.

As I said earlier, once you see your intention to care for yourself as *innocent*, you'll never feel guilty again.

Without changing anything in your external world, your children will sense by your very presence your expanded experience of wholeness and abundance. This gives them permission to stay connected to their own spirit, with its natural flow of abundance. Regardless of the amount of money you may or may not have, children know themselves to be abundant. If we but connect to this place within ourselves as mothers, we provide them the rich environment in which to thrive and manifest their heart's desires.

6

Mutuality—Of Mutual Benefit

"Who you are speaks so loudly, I can't hear a word you say," wrote Emerson. More than anything we say to or do for them, our children pick up on our energy. It's the energy behind our words and actions that speaks the most powerfully.

When we exude a presence of goodness and abundance as the result of restoring our spirit, it makes us feel good inside, and our children feel this. We feel an *enthusiasm* for life—a word derived ultimately from the Greek *en theos*, which refers to "the God inside." We live a God-inspired life.

The word "inspire" also has an interesting origin, coming from the Latin *inspirare*, meaning "to breathe into." Think of someone who inspires you. Aren't they "full of life"? When we are in the presence of such individuals, we too feel inspired, quite apart from anything they say. Just being around them awakens something within us that causes us to want to elevate our own life.

The same holds true for us when we finally let go of the last vestiges of guilt and martyrdom. When we truly care for the precious life we have been given, we touch a deeper realm that enlivens us. Functioning from this realm, we find ourselves bathed in well-being and consequently full to overflowing.

Not only do we find that we take nothing away from anyone else, but we discover actual mutual benefit for everyone concerned, especially our children. We become a beneficial presence to them. The result is that our beneficial presence is like a breath of fresh air, and we enter what I refer to as the state of "mutuality."

Self-Care Is Mutually Beneficial

To illustrate the life-changing power of mutuality, I want to introduce you to Deb, one of my clients who, as an act of self-care, chose to embark on a meditation practice.

Deb had a busy life and needed something doable, nothing too extreme or difficult to implement. Deciding to meditate for ten minutes before her son woke up in the mornings, she also opted to arrive at school to pick him up in the afternoons five minutes before school was dismissed. Additionally, she intended to take five more minutes to meditate just before she began preparing dinner and moved into her evening routine. In other words, she experimented with a total of twenty minutes of meditation spread throughout her day.

When she launched into her meditation practice, Deb was doubtful that a few minutes here and there could really crack the dense energy of the power struggles she and her eight-year-old son, Nate often found themselves in—struggles that sometimes erupted in the blink of an eye.

Not being a morning person, her first few weeks of meditation were horizontal. Still, even the first morning, just waking up ten minutes before Nate and focusing on gratitude, she experienced such a good feeling that it changed her approach to getting him out of bed. Instead of walking into his bedroom, turning on the light, and shaking him awake—something she did every morning—she found herself gently touching his cheek and quietly marveling at this little guy who lay before her. She gazed at his peaceful little body for what seemed like five minutes before, reluctantly, she forced herself to wake him.

"I didn't realize how long it had been since I had touched him so tenderly," Deb shared with me. "The truth is, I hadn't treated him so tenderly in quite some time. The effect of simply touching his cheek stayed with me for the rest of the day. In fact, it's still with me now as I relate the experience to you. I want more of those moments."

Deb was doubly surprised by what happened next. When Nate opened his eyes, instead of turning over as he did every morning, he looked back into his mom's eyes. The feel was so different from their usual mornings that they gazed at each other in silence for what seemed like an eternity. Then they embraced. Neither of them said a word, and yet the silence spoke volumes.

In those precious moments of waking Nate, time stood still. Deb wasn't focused on Nate's toys on the floor or how much there was to get done before leaving for school. Deb was operating "outside" of time, connected to a higher energy and "who she was" set the tone for her son and for their morning.

Deb had become a beneficial presence for Nate. Nourishing her own spirit created a palpably alive atmosphere between them. For Deb, taking care of herself proved *mutually* beneficial for both she and Nate.

Imagine caring for yourself and cultivating a sense of well-being. Without having to say or do anything, you become a beneficial presence just by the fact your child is in your presence.

Also, you are being of benefit to your child in the most important of ways, which is that you are actually *present* with them when you do something like drive them to a baseball game or a dance class. It's this sense of connection that our children most crave. When we are connected within ourselves, we are able to truly connect with our children and others.

"Me" time is Mutually Beneficial

Another client of mine, Lisa, wakes up about thirty minutes before her two children every morning. She makes a latte, sits outside on her glider in her backyard, and does a crossword puzzle. Her backyard is her haven. She has many bird and animal feeders and loves watching the different critters who inevitably come to visit and say good morning. She is in a world beyond her world.

This is Lisa's "me" time. This "me" time ensures her tank is full when her children wake up. *Their* morning routine is enhanced because *she* is full. She is a beneficial presence in her children's world because she makes time to care for herself. In other words, her "me" time is far from selfish. On the contrary, it's mutually beneficial.

I want you to notice that, unlike meditating, there's nothing that looks overtly "spiritual" about Lisa's time for herself. But think back to an earlier chapter in which we discussed spirituality. We said that when we are in touch with our spirit, the whole of life becomes spiritual. For Lisa, her morning latte, sitting in her backyard, and crossword puzzle are spiritual activities because they connect her with her *self.*

Something is spiritual when it comes from your essential self. This is why it's so important not to try to follow someone else's prescription for living a spiritual life. Simply live your life in a manner that's infused with your spirit, and you will be living a spiritual life.

Mutually Beneficial Self-Care Doesn't Have to Cost

I see so many parents who, in an attempt to spend more time with their children, automatically buy into the culture's way of doing so by taking them to the mall to shop for the latest gadget, clothes or jewelry, going to a movie, or on a fancy vacation. We think spending time with them will include spending money on them.

Of course, there's a place for these. But the sad thing is that many parents erroneously believe that this is the necessary roadmap to connection with their children. Parents can be so disconnected from ourselves, and consequently our kids, that even when we go on such activities we experience little if any mutuality. Parent and child just aren't able to be "present" with one another.

The simple fact is, you can't buy mutuality.

Another client of mine, Amy, so wanted to implement self-care in her life, but she just couldn't find either the time or the money. She is a single mom who, on top of her already busy life, works two jobs and is stretched by many outside commitments. How can one engage in self-care in a situation like this?

Amy decided to go for a run after dinner in the evenings. She'd been wanting to lose some weight anyway. Immediately, she felt reconnected with a long-lost love of physical activity and a relationship with her body, whose needs had been all but forgotten. Even that first evening after her run, she felt so energized that she found herself dancing around her kitchen as she did the dishes. When her son, Brian walked into the kitchen, he noticed her good mood and remarked on it. Amy had taken care of her needs and found herself needling nothing from Brian that evening. She simply allowed Brian to be Brian; to do his evening tasks like homework, taking out the trash, emptying the dishwasher, showering, in his own way and in his own timing. No managing, directing or controlling. There was a relaxed and connected quality to their time together that evening. They laughed that they both benefitted from her run!

Did it take Brian a while to complete his tasks? You bet, but complete them he did—in his own way and in his timing. Because Amy was fulfilled within herself, she was dwelling in a highest state of being and felt no need to micromanage Brian's timing. Consequently, he received the good feeling of a job well done. Amy's run liberated them both.

Because Amy worked two jobs, it was a challenge to get herself to run in the evening after a long day's work, and yet she loved the good feeling she got following her run. The afterglow is what kept her going. After some time, her daughter, Alexia asked to go with her. This surprised Amy, as her daughter was fourteen and hadn't been interested in spending any time with her mom, much less going on a run together. Some days they ran in total silence, and other days Alexia shared stories about friends or school. Not only was Amy getting a workout, which gave her more energy throughout her day, but her relationship with her children was shifting. There was a bond. Amy realized how this was so important at this time in Alexia's life, a moment when she trying to find out who she was.

Amy's run wasn't only of benefit to herself, but also to Alexia, since she became a meaningful presence in her daughter's life. This is mutuality.

Nourishing our spirit is attractive, inspiring, contagious, and of benefit not only to ourselves but to those around us. When our own cup is overflowing, our children are the first to benefit.

7

Abundance Is Your Birthright

To feel fulfilled in life is to experience a state of abundance. The very word "fulfilled" means *filled to the full*. There's no sense of scarcity of the things you truly need in order to enjoy your days on earth, no feeling that something is sorely lacking in your life. Filled to the full implies an overflow of enough, both to spare and to share.

Imagine living in a calm state of mind, knowing your every need is met and that choices and opportunities abound. The best definition I've heard of abundance is living in an anxiety-free state. This is everyone's birthright.

Having said this, I want to further emphasize something we touched on earlier, which is that when I speak of abundance, I'm not simply talking about material prosperity. I'm referring principally to your *inner* state, which has a huge impact on your external circumstances. Enough—indeed, abundance—isn't about a large bank account, though it may include this, but is a state of consciousness. If abundance is your inner state, you will feel "enough" regardless of your circumstances. In other words, it's all about your sense of your value—your *intrinsic* worth.

Abundance Begins on the Inside

Underlying a failure to believe in our worth is a mentality of scarcity and lack, which is the mindset most people buy into. This then has the collective effect of creating a world that does in fact experience scarcity, in the forms of hunger, poverty, squalor, and war over a perceived short-age of resources.

Entirely in the shadow is the fact that the mindset of "there isn't enough to go around" is a reflection of our personal belief that "*I* am not enough." Of course, as we have been seeing, this is a failure to know our worth. The scarcity on the planet is a spinoff of our collective personal sense of inadequacy.

The flip side of the belief there isn't enough is the way so many of us buy into the idea that we are "too much." We get told we're too emotion-al, too sensitive, too big for our britches, too laid back, too energetic, and on and on. The consequence of hearing these messages from our early days is that we learn to constrain ourselves. We squeeze ourselves into a box that's far too small, limiting our enjoyment of life, our enthusiasm, our capacity for sharing, and ultimately what we can contribute to the world. Feeling small, we live a life of "playing small."

Did it ever occur to you that the belief there isn't enough, along with the idea that you are sometimes "too much," are two ends of a seesaw? They have nothing to do with who you really are, but are entirely a way of thinking of yourself that comes from being disconnected from your essential being. Right in the center of that seesaw is the fulcrum, which is your inherent worth and value. It's this center point that people are seeking and that the universe is here to help us find.

The Abundant Mother

There is nothing like motherhood to challenge us to embody a sense of abundance in our lives. It seems that there are infinite tasks to be done with only 24 hours in a day to accomplish them. It's so easy to see our children stumbling rather than thriving. With so much to do and the desire to do it well, mothers can easily, even with the strongest of inten-tions fall into a consciousness of lack and fear. Recognizing abundance is an ongoing practice that we can participate in daily. When we become aware we're seeing a situation through the filter of lack, we can train ourselves to look for abundance.

What abundance do I see around me? What abundance can I find around me? Challenge yourself to answer these questions throughout your day. When you take the time to look for the abundance around you, you will find it.

This is why the art of inner-care is tricky. Rather than waiting to feel a sense of abundance, it's the act of taking care of yourself that transforms your experience of lack into one of abundance.

Feeling Like a Million Bucks

There's nothing like self-care to transport us from a mentality of lack to the experience of abundance and worth. My client Jasmine describes the day she made the connection between self-care and abundance:

My own introduction to self-care sometimes felt wobbly, like a baby learning to walk with lots of starts and stops, stumbles and tumbles. Sometimes it felt more like a roller coaster, filled with many ups and downs. Just when I seemed to gain momentum, I'd cave in on myself and fall back to my old ways. It felt so challenging to give myself permission to do something for myself. Yet each time I did, I felt like a million bucks.

There were to be a host of ways I cut corners on myself during the course of a day. Small, seemingly inconsequential things like skipping breakfast, skipping workouts, not drinking water, not washing my face at night, not calling a friend back, letting our bills pile up, or not paying bills and getting unnecessary late fees.

Yet every time I went to the gym, for example, I'd feel great. I'd feel like *myself*. In fact, it was on my way home from the gym one day, when I was literally shouting "woo hoo" out loud in my car, that I realized I wanted to hold on to this feeling. I'd found me. I knew the mother I was going to be that afternoon because of that trip to the gym. I'd made the connection between self-care and child-care, between self-care and abundance. I knew I'd be mothering my son from a place of abundance when I got home.

That day in my car, I decided I would do whatever it takes to feel this way every day. That was the day I got off the roller coaster and committed to feel like a million bucks for myself and my son.

Relating to Our Children from Abundance

When we take the time to let go of all the ways we've seen ourselves as lacking and relate to ourselves through the eyes of our own innate abundance, we change everything about the way we relate to our children. Whereas we have tended to see situations through a lens of lack and fear, we now see that we are all whole, enough, and valuable. This allows us to separate our children's *behavior* from their *being*. Their essence remains intact, even as they make mistakes and learn lessons through their actions. There's nothing more important to building confidence than knowing that learning is a part of life. Seeing themselves as whole, abundant beings who are learning is so drastically different from feeling inherently flawed.

When we see our children through the filter of abundance rather than lack, they feel this. Everything changes about the way they see themselves and their stumbles. Just observe how, when you feel good about who *you* are, your children feel relieved. They are free to feel good about who they are.

8

More than Enough

The foremost challenge faced by mothers I work with as a counselor is that there isn't enough time, support, or money to truly take care of themselves.

Rather than waiting until we perceive ourselves to have enough support, enough time, and enough resources, it has become apparent to me that we must take care of ourselves *first*.

Right in the midst of feeling there's "not enough" time, we must take a contrary position. We must put on a piece of music and dance, take out a paintbrush and paint, or buy a jumprope and jump—if even for only a few minutes. Tending to our spirit is the bridge to the higher state of consciousness we all deserve to enjoy.

From Incremental to Exponential Results

You can see how this works from one of my clients who was a successful television producer but wanted to change careers. Dana regularly worked long days and then went home to care for her two children. As far as she was concerned, self-care wasn't an option. Still, reluctantly, she decided to schedule ten minutes a day to nourish her spirit. I explained that it didn't matter what she did. She could walk her dog in her neighborhood, ride her bike to the park, work in her garden or engage in anything she loved. The one thing that mattered was that she didn't cancel on herself. "All right, ten minutes a day it is," she agreed, "and I promise not to cheat."

At first these ten minutes didn't seem to bring about any noticeable results. She still felt exhausted in her producing job and quite unable to imagine how she would gracefully exit this career and enter something more in alignment with her heart, not to mention less hours so she could spend more time with her children. Little by little though, she began to experience such a good feeling inside herself that she wondered where it was coming from. It was then she realized she had developed the ability to depend on her word to herself. She was able to give herself ten minutes a day, and she could count on herself to do so. This resulted in a healthy sense of pride in herself. She valued her choice to value herself.

After a while, this small payoff of pride over her self-care yielded a compound dividend as Dana found herself feeling more alive. Simultaneously, she was more engaged in her life. The better she felt about herself, the better her relationship was with her children. She complained less. Her children helped out more. Now she was generating the energy and enthusiasm needed to invest in transitioning to a different career—and it was all happening effortlessly, flowing from the rich resources she was discovering as she became increasingly aware of her inner being.

Her children were so supportive of her self-care that they joined in with their own practices, which they lovingly refer to as "family-care." Dana now works with an educational firm and travels often for work. Even on long travel days, she continues to engage in self-care.

Dana's experience contains a wonderful gem—quite a paradox, actually. Last month, she was feeling under the weather, so she took a few days off to rest. The work culture in which she functions doesn't share her value of self-care, and everyone keeps going even though they may feel awful. Well, Dana has cultivated the muscle to rest anyway. Although she's the one who rests the most, she's the highest performer in her division—a fact she attributes to her self-care. She jokes that self-care has gotten her a promotion—the more she takes care of herself, the more money she makes! People, especially mothers, come to her asking her secret, so that what she has learned is now proving valuable not only to her children and her bank account, but to others at work as well.

A Question of Time

Picture yourself doing something you love, such as playing the piano, painting a picture with your child, or hiking in nature. While you are engrossed in such an activity, you may have little if any awareness of time. Why is that?

At such times, it's as if we're outside of time. We leave behind the churning thoughts in our head. Instead, we are simply immersed in the transcendent reality of abundance. We are connected to the eternal moment, in which there's no thought, just awareness. Consequently, we experience no sensation of being rushed.

As mothers, with so many logistics and so much to schedule, we can so easily become locked into thoughts about time, such as, "If my child doesn't come downstairs for breakfast this minute, I'm going to be late for my appointment this morning." In a scenario like this, a sense of panic takes over. In this panicked state, time begins to feel limited, lacking and like a huge burden. We become super aware of practically every second as it passes.

Whenever we are immersed in the ever-present wellspring of our infinitely abundant nature, it brings with it a whole soul payoff of increased physical, mental, and creative energy. Something both relaxes and simultaneously lights up within us when we are connected to this limitless source. And now a rather strange thing happens—we find ourselves frequently arriving on time, accomplishing everything we needed to do in less time than we imagined it would take, and not feeling badly about ourselves on those occasions when our child doesn't come down to breakfast "this minute" or we don't get everything done that was on our list.

When we become more invested in the *quality* of the time that we do have, our relationship with our children is enriched. We are inspired, alive with great ideas, overflowing with creativity. We engage in the same activities, but now from a space of expanded awareness and higher consciousness. In other words, investing ourselves in taking care of our spirit ahead of everything else brings an exponential payoff that feeds into every area of our life, especially life with our children.

My client Esther described a situation with her four-year-old daughter that occurred one morning before they left the house:

I was practicing taking care of myself first in the mornings. I had gotten a new haircut, and as part of my self-care, I was taking the extra time to curl my hair before work. I was feeling so good about my choice. Sarah walked into the bathroom and asked me to curl her hair too. I felt a sense of panic as I heard my inner voice say, "Oh, no. I can't curl your hair too. I can barely curl my own hair. In fact, what in the world am I doing curling my hair? Am I crazy?"

I took a deep breath as I heard an even deeper, perfectly calm voice say aloud, "Of course I'll curl your hair, honey." Her hair was already in a ponytail, so I curled the back of it and off she ran to get dressed. There was a moment of connection between us that wasn't about her hair. It's hard to describe, but in that moment, we experienced each other beyond our morning routine.

The rest of the morning went exceptionally well. I had let go of the need to get to work on time. I knew we might hit more traffic on the way and I let that be okay. Sarah got herself dressed and was happily waiting for me at the front door to go to school and show her teacher her hair.

That simple moment of connection I felt in the bathroom while curling her hair was golden. It lit up the rest of our morning. There was a sparkle in both our eyes that isn't usually there in the mornings. For those few moments, time stood still.

When Self-Care Is *Most* Needed

Over and over again, I see clients begin to experience excellent results from self-care, only to be thwarted as soon as work or family life throw them a curveball. When work becomes super busy or a child gets sick, self-care can be the first thing we allow to fall away. We revert to an old, unconscious pattern that says we aren't enough or don't have enough.

I have learned that the times when self-care seems impossible are the times I actually need to engage in it the *most*. In other words, if I'm buying into a belief in lack, this is precisely when I need to anchor myself in the ever-present abundance of my nature. Belief in lack leaves us feeling disconnected from our life force, whereas the experience of abundance allows us to tap into this exalted state of consciousness precisely when we most need it.

The fact is, life does throw us curveballs—as Simone, the single mother of a nine-year-old, found out. When she began to take better care of herself, it made her feel good to know she was modeling for her son Sammy a "way of being." A kindergarten teacher, she picked up a nasty stomach bug from the school. When Sammy brought her orange juice, doing what he could to help out, Simone smiled. Marveling at his desire to be of assistance, she was nevertheless determined to power through.

When Simone's symptoms didn't improve, she realized she could continue to try to care for both herself and Sammy or she could reach out and ask someone to take Sammy. They had no immediate family in town and asking for assistance wasn't Simone's strong suit because she "didn't want to burden anyone."

Despite the fact Simone made quite a few calls, no one was available to care for Sammy. He, however, had an idea, suggesting that he should ask his teacher to take him to the park. Although Simone was out of options, she felt this would be asking way too much. She also felt it might be inappropriate to impose on a teacher in this way, especially on a Saturday. Nevertheless, because she was out of options, she finally called his teacher, who was more than happy to help out and was over within the hour. Sammy had a wonderful experience at the park, a memory he will cherish for a long while.

The beautiful thing about this story is that when Simone finally broke down and asked for assistance, it opened the way for Sammy to choose his own form of self-care—time at the park with his teacher. When, in a time of need, we override the feeling that we might be "putting people out," we open the way for others to benefit. And, of course, Sammy was only putting into practice what he had seen his mother model.

You Are More Than Enough

Begin to understand yourself as more than enough—that there's nothing wrong with you, nothing damaged, nothing broken. You are not your mistakes, and your life hasn't been a mistake. You are not your past, and not even your own parents' child. You are a unique spirit, a child of the universe, with goodness and gifts in abundance within you.

What would it take to access the abundance at your center and open the floodgates for an overflow? Perhaps it involves waking up just five minutes before your child and appreciating yourself during those extra minutes. Perhaps it's beginning a simple meditation practice such as sitting in stillness. Would becoming involved in a spiritual community benefit you, especially if you need to let go of and replace toxic relationships? Maybe considerably reducing, or if need be abstaining from, alcohol would make a difference.

To commit to a flow of abundance from within your center likely calls for an action that runs contrary to your typical style. For instance, if you are hard on yourself and hold yourself to high standards, perhaps you are being asked to ease up on yourself and relax into life, allowing it to give to you. On the other hand, you may be being called to exercise a greater level of self-discipline or accountability for your intentions and goals. Only you know what's reaching out to you from your inner being, asking of you more for yourself than you've thought possible for your life.

There is no one-size-fits-all approach to transformation, which means we must each choose our own tailor-made transformational curriculum to suit our soul's particular aesthetics and yearning. Commit to taking at least one small inspired action, proving to yourself that who you are isn't in any way lacking.

Meet Your Undefended Self

Why do we struggle with understanding ourselves to be more than enough?

As we grow up, most of us internalize a constricted way of seeing ourselves. We buy into the narrow view of ourselves inherited from our family, society, and humanity in general, believing this is "how life is supposed to be." This becomes our identity, our worldview.

Some of us react to the way society crushes our true self as we are growing up by becoming afraid, negative, limited in our scope. We feel like we're "no one." It's not that there's actually something deficient about us. It's what we've been told about ourselves and how we've come to see ourselves that's the problem. Others react by becoming grandiose, with an inflated ego, determined to prove we are "someone." Whether we develop poor self-esteem or an inflated feeling of self-esteem, most of us don't grow up to be the unique individual each of us inherently is. When we live our life "coping," "surviving"—or as I often hear people say, "getting by" or "doing okay"—what we are seeing is simply layer upon layer of self-protection covering up our underlying, untouched, original self—a self that has been there all along.

Whether it manifests as feeling small or acting grandiosely, the desire for more—and to *be* more—is in its essence a longing to uncover and express our original self in all its greatness. Feeling small or acting grandiosely are both just masks, hiding the fact we've lost touch with the core of our being. Once we access this core and allow it to flourish, it will transform every aspect of our life—especially life with our children.

Cultivating an awareness of prosperity, bounty, and abundance is to flow with the mighty tide of the evolving universe. But just like learning to float on a current, it can require a little practice. With steady practice at seeing things differently, the mindset of lack and scarcity we have taken on in the survival state we learned growing up shifts to a blossoming of a more accurate reflection of our true nature and the real state of things.

When it comes down to it, at any given moment we are either looking at our life through the filter of lack or through the filter of abundance. Change the filter and you will transform your life.

9

Who Are You Really?

The Lebanese artist, philosopher, and author Kahlil Gibran brings a different perspective to what it means to birth a child into the world. He challenges us to cut the cord of thinking that our children belong to *us*. Take a moment to read through Gibran's wise words regarding our children:

Your children are not your children

They are the daughter or son of Life's longing for Itself.

They came through you, but not from you

Though they are with you, they belong not to you

You may give them your love, but not your thoughts

For they have their own thoughts

You may house their body, but not their soul

For their soul dwells in the house of tomorrow, which you can not visit, not even in your dreams.

Our children have their own soul, which is individualized and equal to our own. Not only do they not belong to us, but their soul dwells in the house of tomorrow, meaning that their life isn't one we can actually control. Despite what we may desire for them, they will be who they will be.

The consequence of this insight is that our children serve a different purpose in our life than most of us have imagined. *We* think we are here to bring our children up, but this is only part of the equation. Our children are also here to assist *us* to develop more fully into the person we essentially are.

The journey of motherhood is an evolutionary path that takes us to the heart of our true self and our children are our best guides. We've all heard the saying, "It takes a village to raise a child." Michael Bernard Beckwith, when performing christenings, says, "It take a child to raise a village." I like to say that *I'm being evolved by my child.*

One reason children can do this is that, though we may have a wealth of life experience, this can never outweigh the reality that a child is closer to its soul identity, largely unaffected by the limitations society places on us as we grow up.

Have you ever thought about the fact that your child's soul knows everything it needs to know for this life's journey? Imagine what your life might be like today had you been encouraged to retain your original soul identity, rather than taking on an identity shaped largely by others.

Just as our children don't belong to us, neither did we belong to our parents. We came through them, but we are not of them. We have our own soul identity, hidden from our awareness though it may be. For this reason, I rewrote part of Gibran's poem from the perspective of a child. You might wish to read it aloud. Many find it to be a freeing exercise:

My parents are not my parents.

I am the daughter (or son) of Life's longing for Itself.

I came through them, but not from them

Though I was with them, I belong not to them

They may have given me their love, but not their thoughts

For I have my own thoughts

They may have housed my body, but not my soul

For my soul dwells in the house of tomorrow, which they cannot visit, not even in their dreams.

What Gibran is saying is especially helpful in the case of a person who has grown up believing themselves to be less than they truly are. For instance, no matter how many classes my client Randy took, how many books he read, how hard he tried, he couldn't seem to find a way to let go of the stain he perceived on his soul because he believed himself to be unwanted.

Randy's parents were teenagers who were drunk at a party when he was conceived. Taking the time to really be present with this poem proved freeing for him. Whereas he had struggled for years with trying not to think of himself as the product of an unwanted pregnancy, the poem allowed him to see what he *is* the product of—life's longing for itself.

Remember the words, "They may have housed his body, but not his soul"? When Randy caught the importance of these words, he reconnected with his original soul identity and for the first time in his life felt at home within himself. His experienced his soul as free and unencumbered at last.

Come Home to Yourself

In *Anam Cara: A Book of Celtic Wisdom,* the Irish poet John O'Donohue writes, "To be holy is to be home, to be able to rest in the house of belonging that we call the soul." To be holy, is to know ourselves to be whole.

Our calling is to come home to *ourselves.*

This is such a liberating insight because it allows us to be free of our biological conditioning, as well as free of the burden of painful past experiences. Whatever we perceive our childhood did to us, and whatever may have befallen us since, none of this has to do with who we actually *are.*

All the ways in which we have been conditioned by family, the wider society, and the things that have happened to us can't affect our essence, our core, our very being. No amount of conditioning has the power to touch our center. It can only affect the way we think about ourselves and the emotions we experience around this.

Imagine for a moment that you were born in a different country to different parents. You would have been brought up to speak a different language perhaps, with different cultural values, different family values, more money or less money. Still, deep in your center, you would be intact. This is because there is a *you* that transcends your biology, language, and culture. This transcendent self has been within you all along, though covered up by your own misperceptions about yourself.

If we live out our life identifying ourselves as the "child" of someone, we will exist in a constricted mode, living according to *their* rules about how life is to be navigated. But if we are daughters and sons of the universe, of the life force, for whom our parents were but temporary delivery vehicles, then we need to nurture our own unique identity. At the same time, we will be cognizant of the fact that the family we came through provided us with the circumstances we needed to live the life we came here to live. We can be grateful for whatever we may have received from them without being held captive to what we didn't receive from them but felt we should have.

Especially as mothers, there are all kinds of demands on us to take care of the necessities of everyday life. We're trying to do the right things for our children—send them to the right schools, enroll them in the right activities—when it's actually liberating to recognize that our house of belonging is our soul and not these activities. When we begin to rest in our soul identity more than an identity of "doing" for our children, we can help our children remain connected to their soul identity.

Do You Believe in Your Intrinsic Worth?

Over the eighteen years I've been in private practice, I have come to see that although we all experience unique circumstances and events, many of us share a common core belief that we are not deserving or worthy, flawed, perhaps even damaged—and maybe even broken. A belief that we are flawed at our core keeps us feeling separate from our true soul identity and our good.

As we saw earlier, it comes down to whether we understand ourselves in terms of our *being* or in terms of our *doing*, original sin or original innocence.

The word "sin" is a term used anciently in archery and refers to missing the bull's eye, literally "missing the mark." We have mistakenly equated "making a mistake" with the idea that when we do, something is wrong with us. This is because we have confused who we *are* with the things we *do*.

We will "miss the mark" in life many times, just like a child stumbles when learning to walk or drops the ball in a game of catch. Our children will miss the mark many times in their lifetime, sometimes many times in a day! What isn't true is that because we miss the mark, there's something wrong with us. Our only sin, if we choose to use the term, is that we *believe* there's something wrong with us, which is why we end up doing things that betray our true nature. In other words, how you *see* yourself is to a large extent how you will *be*.

The relevance of this to raising a child—and, in fact, to raising ourselves—is so profound that it can change our entire relationship with our children, their relationship with themselves and consequently, the way they will be in the world. We are seeking to recover a sense of ourselves as essentially good and whole with nothing wrong, broken, damaged or lacking. At the same time, we want to allow our children to stay connected to their intrinsic goodness, the wonderfulness we recognized in them the first time we looked at them.

Imagine how you would feel about yourself if you thought of yourself as intrinsically good. Imagine your relationship with your children if you imagined them as intrinsically good. Then imagine the impact upon the world with each of us acting from our intrinsic goodness.

If we don't clear our vision, we will remain in a victim mentality interminably. We will constantly feel we are journeying uphill, doing it all alone, a martyr to motherhood. Despite our best intentions to raise our children differently from how we were raised, we can't help but pass this mentality to them by osmosis. No matter what we teach them to the contrary, they will pick up how we really feel about ourselves from our moods, our vibes, our very presence. This is how our original sin of not feeling adequate, not loving ourselves, not caring for ourselves in the way we deserve, is transmitted from generation to generation.

We can only pass on to our children what we ourselves have come to know as an everyday reality. This is why it's so important to understand how truly good we are. Embodying our own goodness is pivotal to enriching our life and thereby providing a context in which our children and entire family can find fulfillment.

My client Jane experienced daily power struggles with her son Joshua. In an attempt to raise him to be a polite, well-educated young man, daily she drew his attention to his manners, chores that needed doing, and his study habits. When he disregarded what she was trying to teach him, rebelling, what had been well-intended on her part escalated into bickering and quarreling.

As Jane gradually became aware of her choice of words and tone of voice when speaking to Joshua, she noticed she made statements that pointed out what he *wasn't* doing rather than what he *was* doing. Instead of engaging and encouraging him, she was criticizing him.

This discovery perplexed her. How could she encourage him without pointing out behavior he needed to improve? She didn't want to have to coddle a fourteen-year-old. She wanted him to rise up and take responsibility for himself.

As we explored how her manner with Joshua reflected the way she related to herself, Jane began to see how hard she was on herself—how, with seemingly good intentions, she continually pointed out to herself what she was doing wrong rather than what she was doing well. When she looked deeper, she found a woman who believed herself to be seriously flawed.

Raised by an extremely critical father, Jane lost her sense of her own innocence early in life. She continually sought to prove to her father that she was worthy of his praise. Instead, he constantly criticized her, making it clear that he didn't trust her to make good choices for herself. Consequently, Jane came to believe she was broken and needed to be fixed. Just being herself simply wasn't enough.

When Jane began to understand that she couldn't impart a sense of soulful well-being to Joshua when she didn't possess such within herself, she embarked on an experiment. For the next week, she wouldn't point out any of Joshua's shortcomings. When she felt the urge to point something out to him, she instead went into another room and asked herself how this related to the way she criticized *herself.*

Jane also asked herself what she most wished her father had said to her when she was growing up. "What I most wanted to hear," she shared with me, "was that I was okay, that I was enough exactly the way I was, that I could relax and be myself, that I didn't have to prove anything to him. I wanted him to see me, accept me, and love me for me."

Jane suddenly saw that Joshua simply wanted to know that his mother saw him and that he was worthy in her eyes. Consequently, she began telling both herself and Joshua the things she had so wanted to hear from her own father.

Taking a few moments each day, she placed her hand over her heart and connected with herself in the way she had so wished her father could have related to her. As she did so, she said simple things to herself like, "I see you," allowing these words to quench her thirsty heart. She found at least three things each day to notice and value about *herself.*

As Jane practiced this for herself, she also looked silently into Joshua's eyes, sharing three specific things she valued in him during the course of his day. They were things like, "I noticed how patient you were with your little brother at the movie today." Or, "I noticed your persistence throughout your baseball season this spring." More than the actual words she spoke, she focused on the energy with which she said them, making sure to connect with her eyes and heart.

When Jane looked into Joshua's eyes, more often than not she experienced not only her fourteen-year-old son, but also a seven-year-old, a four-year-old, a three-month-old, and his innocent essence all at once, as her gaze peeked straight through to his soul.

What Jane didn't expect was the way Joshua seemed to soak up her words. Over time, she noticed him becoming more talkative in the car on the way home from school in the afternoons. He also stopped rushing back into his room after dinner, instead engaging in conversation about his day and his friends. She felt so much better about the way she was relating to both herself and her son. As she described it, "It feels like a breath of fresh air has entered our relationship."

There is nothing more meaningful and transformative than reconnecting with our own intrinsic sense of goodness, wholeness, value and worth. This is a daily practice that grows over time into deeper intimacy, bonding and connection within ourselves and with our children. We wanted this sense of connection with our parents and I assure you, your children are seeking a deep connection with you, regardless of their behaviors to the contrary.

10

A View from the Mountaintop

Albert Einstein shared a valuable insight, which is that we can't solve problems at the same level of consciousness that created them. Whenever we face a challenging life situation, if we are to find solutions, we need to come from a different perspective.

Self-care can sometimes feel daunting, even when all is going well in our lives. What does caring for our inner life look like when things are challenging? I call this "emotional self-care."

When my clients are facing a difficult situation, I take them through a process I call going to "the mountaintop." Whenever we look at any situation from a higher altitude, we are able to see things through an expanded lens. We move from the filter of lack and limitation to the infinite field of abundance and possibility.

I'd like to share with you how the mountaintop works. Ramona, a client of mine, is a single mother of a beautiful daughter, Betsy. I first met her a year ago when she was struggling following an ugly divorce. Wrestling with intense feelings of betrayal, abandonment, and disappointment, this was nothing like the life she had envisioned for herself and Betsy. To top it off, her husband had moved out of the country, which meant her prospects for receiving child support were grim. Ramona and Betsy were experiencing daily power struggles and just couldn't seem to connect. Their relationship was adversarial regardless of how hard Ramona tried to stay calm.

When I first began encouraging Ramona to nourish her spirit, she practically laughed out loud. Her spirit was the last thing on her list, even though she felt such a longing in her heart for a connection to something more meaningful than her experience of life in her present dire straits.

I had Ramona close her eyes and imagine herself high up on the side of a beautiful mountain looking down upon her life. From this elevated view, she could observe herself grappling with the myriad of emotions she had been left with in the wake of her divorce. As she surveyed the scene that appeared in her imagination, she became aware of just how angry she was at her former husband for leaving. Slowly, she also came to see that, beneath her rage, she blamed herself for the demise of their relationship.

I suggested she climb a little higher, ascending to the top of the mountain now. In her mind's eye, as she steadily gained altitude, looking down upon herself, she realized she was continuing a pattern of self-judgment and self-abandonment—indeed, self-*betrayal*—that was familiar to her from her mother's life.

Looking down, she recognized herself as a young mother, overwhelmed with a sense of responsibility, desperately needing to provide for her daughter, Betsy, by somehow reassembling the pieces of her seemingly broken family life. From this high perspective, Ramona could also see herself as a young child in the midst of her own broken family. She found herself feeling so much empathy for Betsy and what she might be feeling.

As Ramona pondered the scene beneath her, she found herself recalling the sense of wholeness and "all is well" she had experienced as a very young child, before her family had broken up. A feeling of longing welled up within her, and she remembered clearly now the sense of inner "knowing" that had seemed so natural to her as a child but had long been forgotten.

As the task of rebuilding her life got underway, this young mother started to incorporate acts of self-care into her life—simple things such as playing music in the mornings in her home. Betsy watched with glee as her mother sang and danced while preparing eggs for breakfast.

I need you to know that as simple as it is to turn on a little music, until now Ramona had been so preoccupied with the need to support Betsy that she could hardly entertain such an act of self-care. She only saw how she could engage in a measure of self-care when I commented, "You know, putting some music on doesn't cost anything, and neither does it take any extra time, since you're making breakfast anyway."

Playing music in the home led Ramona to another form of self-care. As she began to feel more relaxed and, at times, even joyful despite her circumstances, she found herself feeling so much more connected to Betsy, thoroughly enjoying her daughter's company. Now, when Betsy was coloring on the weekends, Ramona drew alongside her, using this as a time for recharging her batteries, drawing being such a right brained activity.

As Ramona experienced the benefits of doing these little things for herself, she decided that, even though she was on an extremely tight budget, she would take an art class at a local school. Her simple drawings quickly blossomed into full-on sketches, and she began to enthusiastically anticipate the times when she and Betsy sat down together to draw.

Over time, Ramona got in the habit of taking out her sketchpad in the evenings after work. Little did she know, but something as simple as drawing with her daughter reignited within her a passion she had all but forgotten from her days in high school, a love of design. Back then, she had actually thought about going to art school for college, though she didn't in the end because her father deemed her not really serious about it. Instead, he encouraged her to find something more practical so she would be able to support herself if necessary.

Contemplating applying to art school as an adult, Ramona assembled a portfolio of her designs. At this point, the self-doubt she had internalized from her father reared its head. Was she serious enough about her pastime to pursue it as a career? Grappling with her self-doubt left over from high school, she decided to apply anyway. After all, she had nothing to lose. Not only was she accepted, but she was awarded a full scholarship, which was critical given that she was rebuilding her life as a single mom. Today, Ramona is a working single mother and student in a field she adores. Most of all, she feels closer and more connected with Betsy than ever. They share a love of art and design and being together.

It was in viewing her life from the mountaintop that Ramona came to see how she had neglected caring for her spirit. Because of her preoccupation with providing financially for Betsy, she had been afraid to risk anything that might appear to be a distraction or wouldn't pan out into something practical. Yet the truth was that she had been robbing the two of them of the quality of life that drawing with her daughter had sparked within her. As she moved from fear and limited choices to an expanded experience of abundance and possibilities, she was able to break the chains of her past and give herself permission to pursue her own path.

Today, because Ramona nourishes her spirit, she is thriving from the inside out and has created an intimate, connected, and mutually respectful relationship with Betsy that she never experienced with her own parents. As Ramona respects herself by caring for her spirit, she models this respect for Betsy. Indeed, their eyes light up when they see each other.

A New Path Opens Up

From the mountaintop, our perspective changes. We rise up instead of being bogged down by issues. We look down and see our circumstances in a different light.

One reason for this is that we enter into an expanded, even *transcendent,* consciousness, which offers us infinite potential. After all, there's no ceiling on a mountaintop. The sky truly is the limit. From this perspective, we discover before us a whole range of possibilities that we have, until now, been unable to access.

Another client, Becky, a married mother of three, was an executive at a high-end technology corporation. At the top of her game both financially and in terms of her place on the corporate ladder, she came to me because she had a longing within her to shift careers. However, the thought of letting go of the income and security associated with her current job frightened her. The affluence her career provided meant she lived in a beautiful home in a nice neighborhood, while at the same time she was also able to travel and see the world with their children—an aspect of her life that was important to her.

Complicating the picture was the fact there was also much that Becky enjoyed about her job. She liked interacting with experts in the field. Plus, she had met her husband in this industry. It is easy to see how she grappled with letting go, for she assumed that, if she started over as an entrepreneur, it would mean giving up the lifestyle she sincerely wanted for her family.

When Becky closed her eyes and imagined herself high on a mountaintop looking down on her life, she saw herself comfortable in her career, with no real outer crisis. At the same time, she was inwardly unfulfilled. She sensed a yearning within her to feel that her life had meaning—that she was contributing to the world. Quite a dilemma—and, I might add, a common one.

From the higher perspective of the mountain, Becky was able to recognize in herself a scared young girl afraid to move into the unknown, terrified of trusting herself because she was so frightened of making a mistake. Seeing herself in this plight, she began to experience compassion for herself as someone who was doing the best she could. As she watched herself searching for the courage to make a big change in her life, she felt such empathy.

Then came a pivotal moment. Some weeks later, as Becky again visited the mountaintop, it suddenly became clear to her that she truly wanted her children to see their mother as a person who was both thriving and living with a sense of purpose. From that moment on, the decision she had struggled with made itself, and her new path opened up before her.

Becky is building her new business and couldn't be happier. She has a purpose and her days are filled with meaning. She loves her work. Even in these beginning stages of a new business, she is filled with inspiration. She feels so proud of herself and she brings this enthusiasm into her daily life with her family. Her husband and children are so supportive of her choice and she feels wonderful about finding the courage to take the steps to be true to herself.

11

The Emotional Messenger System

"The wound is the place where the Light enters you," said Rumi.

Emotions are greatly misunderstood in our culture, especially where raising our children is concerned. Most of us have been taught to avoid our true emotions at any cost. Some of us also become addicted to various substances in order to avoid feeling. Even when we know we ought to enter into our feelings, most of us only tolerate them in the hope they'll go away.

Add to our avoidance of our feelings the challenge of trying to communicate with our children, significant other, or anyone when charged emotions are present, and you have a recipe for disaster. The fact is, few of us have cultivated effective ways to process our feelings, which is why we become so reactive. We spew our reactions onto our children because we haven't been taught effective ways to calm our own storms.

More than anything else, our inability to effectively handle upset with our children gets in the way of our relationship, connectedness, and intimacy with them. Because we haven't learned to be present with our own inner upset, we allow our emotions to erupt all over our children. When we begin to take ownership for our own emotional reactions, everything about our relationship with our children can change for the better. This is the practice of emotional self-care, caring for our emotional inner-self.

Turning within to care for our own discontent isn't comfortable, and we therefore tend to avoid the very thing that will bring us peace and, ultimately, the connection we're seeking within ourselves and with our children. Yet I've learned that these emotional elements within us, which sometimes seem so dark and intense, are actually messengers.

In a sense, our emotions are like children. They seek our attention because they have something to tell us. Consequently, the more we resist them, the louder they tantrum; whereas if we embrace them, they can be soothed.

Intense emotions such as anger, and even rage, are simply messages that have been seeking our attention for a long time but that we have ignored. For instance, the anger we experience was once a whisper, then a shout, and has finally morphed into an all-out battle cry.

We usually end up in an all-out battle with our children because we don't know how to make peace with the emotions within ourselves. Think about yourself when you are upset with your child. When emotions and reactions are present we usually end up with two "tantrum-ing" children in a room, rather than an adult and a child because we haven't been taught how to process our own emotions effectively.

This was the case with my client Amanda and her two children. It seemed that no matter how many times Amanda told herself she wasn't going to shout at her twins, she failed miserably, yelling at them, then feeling such remorse and shaming herself for falling down yet one more time. "I felt like the worst mother," she confided. "I could see in their eyes the damage I was doing. I could literally see their spirits shrink as I overpowered them with my voice and energy. It was as if the intensity of my voice dimmed the light in their eyes. Little by little, I could see them retreat into themselves."

I asked Amanda why some of us are able to stay calm and collected when our children don't listen to us, whereas others of us are reactive and explosive. As we explored this question, Amanda explained how she felt justified in raising her voice when her children didn't listen to her, even though she hated the feeling that arose within her whenever she exploded at them. After all, she reasoned, if they would only listen, she wouldn't need to raise her voice.

When I explained that how we relate to our children's behavior reflects our own internal environment, Amanda couldn't at first understand how her anger with her children was a reflection of her own relationship with herself. The whole thing seemed quite confusing to her, until I pointed out how Rumi suggests our reactions need to be seen as a wound seeking the light.

As Amanda began to explore the explosion that happened within when her children didn't listen to her, she heard a voice inside shouting, "How dare you not listen to me! How dare you just walk away from me when I'm talking! How dare you just throw me away like an old rag! Am I that dirty? That insignificant?" The voice wasn't Amanda speaking to her children. It was herself shouting at her own father.

Sobbing, Amanda recollected the tender little girl, wounded by her father all those years ago when he simply left the room whenever he didn't like what she had to say to him. Without a word, he just stormed off, leaving her with emotions far too complex for a little girl of six to handle on her own.

Now at last Amanda realized that her anger had been with her long before her children were born. In fact, her children were helping her wounds find the light. She saw how years of unexpressed anger toward her father was being vented on her own children whenever they didn't listen to her.

It was a shock to Amanda to realize that she treated herself exactly as her father had treated her. The consequence was that her mind was a war zone, as she constantly battled herself and her decisions.

Amanda learned to listen to herself, as well as to treat herself with dignity, kindness, and respect. When her children didn't listen to her, she discovered the value of waving a white flag and calling for a truce instead of erupting. Learning to call a truce and create peace within herself was what she needed to do in order to create peace with her children and in her home.

There is no better care for our children than our own emotional self-care. No one benefits more from our emotional self-care than our children.

Since the message in an emotion that has now become a battle cry was present all along, how much better for everyone, not least our own health, that we heed it as soon as it comes to our attention and not try to push it away. If we can catch it when it's still a whisper, all the better. On a larger scale, the warning signs of what ultimate escalates into a school shooting or the outbreak of war between nations were also there all along.

Once we receive the message that a particular emotion is attempting to deliver, the intensity of the energy dissipates. Do you see what a mistake it is to try to get emotions to go away? It's significant that they persist, not quieting down until their message has been delivered.

Don't Judge Your Emotions

Although we tend to categorize emotions as either good or bad, positive or negative, they are neither. They also don't define us. When we take the time to look down from the mountaintop, we realize that who we are is larger than our emotions. They are something we experience, not who we are. They are our body's communication system, alerting us to what's happening inside us.

Emotions are simply energy in motion. They bring our unconscious aspects to our awareness so we can turn the spotlight on them, which enables us to use the energy in ways that serve us, rather than the energy using us. As a friend of mine says, we need to *use* our head instead of *losing* our head.

Even the most painful emotions are here to deliver insights to assist our development. For this reason, rather than moving away from the often strong emotions our children trigger in us, we need to move toward them and welcome the insight they seek to impart. This untangles the knot of entangled energy.

Imagine a crying child. The child seeks our warm embrace and a safe emotional landing site. Well, our painful emotions can be seen as orphaned children in need of our adoption so that we can care for them with compassion.

Compassion is the container that can safely house every emotion if we but provide it. To contain an emotion with compassion means we neither suppress it nor act it out. We simply sit with it without judgment, quietly witnessing ourselves, accepting ourselves and loving ourselves in our emotional state. By observing the emotion and soothing ourselves, we allow the underlying message in the emotion to reveal itself. We can then act on the message, not the emotion. Again, we use our head instead of losing it. We're then able to "talk it out" rather than "act it out."

We are multidimensional beings, able to embrace a fierce emotion and simultaneously feel compassion. It's really no different from the way we are able to provide love to a crying child. Our love embraces the child's tears. We can also feel compassion for ourselves even as we experience anger. This is because the energy of love is far more encompassing than the energy of even the most intense emotion.

With this in mind, love your emotion like it's a fragile infant within you. Wrap your compassion around it as if it were an innocent child with a golden message for you. But notice that I said "love" your emotion, in the sense of feeling compassion for yourself in what you are experiencing, not "indulge" your emotion. Acting emotion out, indulging it, doesn't help you integrate the energy. On the contrary, it's like a muscle—the more you work it, the stronger it becomes.

Again, this is easiest to do when you imagine yourself at the top of a mountain looking down at what you're experiencing. From this lofty perspective, you're more able to see yourself through compassionate eyes. As you practice seeing yourself through compassionate eyes, you will begin to see your child's emotions through compassionate eyes as well.

Getting to the Roots of Emotional Discomfort

Our children stir up the deep, unhealed emotions that are bound up with the hurt we all carry within us. This can be vexing—unless we understand that the reason they get stirred up is so that we can address the emotion and heal the hurt that's behind it. Did you ever think of your children as doing you a favor when they stir these things up? Well, they are.

If you try to avoid the discomfort of the hurting aspects of yourself when they surface, you'll inevitably either project your emotions outward, spewing them all over your children, or you'll try to stuff them down inside yourself, with consequences both psychological and physical.

Although it may not appear so, all the emotions that get stirred up in you toward your children reflect your own inner unrest. What this means is that when you are upset with your child—or anyone in your life, the conflict you are caught up in with the person is a mirror of some aspect of your own inner self that's troubled.

Whenever I find myself upset at my child, or someone or something externally, I need only feel the energy and I can see that there is upset within me. Even if the other party is upset as well, I need only check my own body, my own energy, and it becomes undeniable that there's upset within *me*.

We only ever criticize or blame our children for how we are feeling if we haven't yet discovered that our reaction to them is really about our personal internal state. We are acting out our internal reality. How can I say this? How can judging another be a judgment on myself?

If we feel connected to our own deeper being, this connectedness can't help but cause us to care for ourselves. We have compassion for ourselves, seeing our weaknesses not as failures but as part of the process of self-discovery. It's akin to when a flower begins to bloom. All the petals don't open at once. This isn't an inadequacy, but simply a stage in the evolution and eventual full blossoming of the flower. There's no judgment when we feel connected to ourselves because compassion trumps judgment when we see ourselves in a state of blossoming.

On the other hand, if we don't feel connected to our own being and are therefore critical of ourselves, judging ourselves to be inadequate, how can we possibly feel connected to our children and appreciate them for where they are on their journey? Whenever we don't feel connected to our child and therefore lack compassion for them, it reflects a failure to feel our own connectedness. It mirrors our lack of compassion for ourselves at whatever stage of blossoming we find ourselves in. We then judge others because we judge ourselves.

Does judgment serve a purpose? Indeed it does. Judgment is a call for *compassion*. Instead of being cause to put another person down, feelings of judgment arise in order to awaken our capacity for compassion, first and foremost compassion for ourselves.

The simple fact is that compassion can't coexist with a critical spirit. If we really connect with our child, seeing them for who they are and where they are on their journey, we will automatically feel compassion for them. Judging them pales in the light of caring for them. This is especially the case with mothers, who have an innate gift for compassion and the connectedness it feeds.

Our own compassion is the light that our wounds are seeking.

Become a Container of Compassion for Yourself

The beauty of this is that every emotional situation with our children functions as a barometer of our internal world, which makes our emotional reactions useful when it comes to addressing the unresolved pain within ourselves.

Once I recognize it as *my* upset, *my opportunity to clear something within myself,* I can see it as something that's *for* me, not against me. So it is that I move toward it, not away from it, showing compassion instead of judging. To move away from it would be like moving away from childbirth because it's painful. Instead, we recognize that any discomfort we experience is calling us deeper into our own self-compassion.

Pain is a natural part of life. As we mature emotionally, we recognize that discomfort doesn't kill us. On the contrary, it's when we resist pain that we suffer, since it has a tendency to become our whole focus. By releasing our need to avoid pain, we free ourselves to receive the gifts life seeks to share with us through the painful times. We are then able to take full responsibility for our experiences and reactions, using them all for our growth so that we might create more connected relationships with our children.

Conflicts with our children frequently involve intense emotion. However, when we identify and come to peace with the discord in ourselves, such conflicts tend to die down. For this reason, much as we might not like to think so, turning away from the charged interactions with our children and focusing instead on the dissonance within our own being is the most effective way to address our emotional pain.

When we take this approach, we more readily find ourselves connecting with our children, relating to them with compassion, able to create the intimate relationship with them that we so desire and they so desire with us. Viewed in this way, our children are assisting us to consciously evolve our own life so that we may be the individuals that we came to be, reaching the full potentiality that makes us feel so alive and on purpose.

Emotion Seen from the Mountaintop

In this context, I think of Joanna and her three children. When it came time to do homework, conflict seemed to erupt between Joanna and one or more of the kids practically every evening. She particularly seemed to end up in yelling matches with her twelve-year-old son Joey.

It would start innocently enough, with Joanna simply asking what assignments he had due for the next day. As she attempted to get him to start an assignment, let alone complete it, her anxiety mounted. Becoming frustrated and finally angry, she blamed him for being such a "procrastinator." Night after night the scene was repeated, making evenings a thoroughly unpleasant experience for everyone.

In one of our sessions together, I had Joanna go up to the mountaintop to witness her emotional life, and particularly this pattern, from a higher perspective. From this vantage point, she was able to look down at herself and feel the intense frustration she experienced whenever she was locked in battle with her children. She felt her muscles tighten, her throat become constricted, her jaw clench, her stomach knot. How was it possible to become so uptight all because of such a simple evening routine?

From the mountaintop, Joanna also saw her exceedingly stressful life. For a start, she was in the middle of a messy divorce. Between taking three children to three different sets of activities, working full-time, and performing the tasks required to run a home and care for her children, she hardly had a moment to herself. Given her situation, what chance was there to process the feelings she had about her divorce, much less her feelings about her child's homework?

At times Joanna was so overwhelmed that she felt she couldn't even pause to get a glass of water for herself. Consequently, by evening time, when homework was calling out, she was exhausted. As she viewed this aspect of herself from the altitude of the mountain, she saw herself in survival mode, functioning like a drill sergeant.

Then, in a flash of insight, Joanna unexpectedly found herself looking down at herself not as a grown woman and mother but as a ten-year-old girl. There she was, suiting up with the very same armor she herself wore now around her own children.

One of three children herself, Joanna recalled how she often seemed to need that suit of armor when her father came home from work in the evenings. A sensitive child, she was forever trying to anticipate his moods, strategizing about how to avoid his tirades. Even when she had done her best to accommodate his every whim, his temper still flared. And if she got upset, this particularly irked him, for he couldn't stand it when she allowed her sensitivity to show. At such times, he became preoccupied with helping her to "toughen up."

Only now, as she looked down at her present life from the mountaintop, as well as on herself as a vulnerable little girl of ten, could Joanna at last experience compassion for herself. Moved by the scene before her, she felt her heart crack wide open, forming an all-encompassing container of compassion—for herself. All these years, it had seemed to her that if only she had been stronger, her father would have loved her the way she longed to be loved. Now at last she could see how mistaken she was to have held herself responsible for his behavior, as if in some way his anger was her fault.

Can you imagine living your life feeling flawed at your core? As Joanna began to see how she had perceived herself to be inherently defective—as if her very *being here* was a mistake—she found herself sobbing. As her tears flowed, layer upon layer of self-criticism, shame, disappointment, regret, and rage began washing away. How much energy she had invested in covering up her perceived flaws, not realizing that hiding them kept her from the close connection she was seeking all along.

Embrace *All* of Who You Are

Now I'm going to ask you to take in one of the most amazing paradoxes. I want you to think about all those parts of yourself you've felt embarrassed about, the parts you wish you could get rid of, and especially the feeling that *you* are somehow "wrong"—that you shouldn't *be* the person you are. Can you imagine loving these very parts of yourself? Can you imagine that these are the very parts of yourself that you have orphaned, and now so desperately need to be adopted and loved? Can you see yourself holding these parts up to the light and, instead of rejecting them, treasuring them?

The places that you deem the least attractive within you are the places that need your love the *most*.

As Joanna increasingly caught onto this and began to do it, she was able to *love herself back to herself*. Over time, she learned to embrace the parts of her that seemed so utterly imperfect. She realized these were the aspects of herself that most needed her love, and that to love such a shamed part of herself is what love is really all about.

In my experience as a counselor, almost everyone tries to bypass this step. People want to get rid of the very aspects of themselves they most need to embrace.

Going to the mountaintop and embracing the hurting places within her now became a regular practice of emotional self-care in Joanna's life. Then, one day, something quite startling happened. For the first time, she saw *beneath* her perceived defects, right to her core. There before her eyes was a little girl of pure innocence, her authentic self. To meet herself again for the first time since her earliest years was a true homecoming.

Finding compassion for all of the different aspects of herself allowed the layers of protection Joanna had amassed to fall away, one after the other. Finding herself to be a beautiful, sensitive, openhearted girl, she not only softened to herself but also to her children, especially Joey. Sometimes at night she went into his bedroom like she used to when he was a baby. As she now saw her own innocence, she practiced seeing his.

One evening before dinner, Joey was playing basketball outside. As Joanna looked out of the window, the thought occurred to her, "Of course he doesn't want to come in and do his homework. Why would he, when he's been sitting at a desk all day at school? He needs a little time to himself." The compassion she had learned to feel for herself welled up toward her son.

That evening Joanna made Joey a cup of hot chocolate and listened as he complained about how he disliked homework. Instead of judging him, she joined in, sharing with him how, after a long day at work, she sometimes just wanted to come home and watch television. Reaching over to her, he placed his hand on hers. Strangely, nothing had changed, and yet everything had changed. Joey still doesn't like doing homework. The difference is that Joanna feels more connected to herself and therefore, to Joey than ever before.

If you are to lead a fulfilling life in which you can really connect with your children, the crucial step is to see yourself from the top of the mountain. Once you glimpse yourself as you *truly* are, without all the false, limiting things you have believed about yourself, you will undergo a shift from feeling shameful, disconnected, full of regret, and all the self-rejection that has bound you.

Seeing yourself from the mountaintop, you actually begin to feel love for the parts of yourself over which you experience the greatest embarrassment—the parts you wish were different and that have caused you to so devalue yourself that you may well feel utterly undeserving of a different life from the one you're living. Being able to embrace, to love, and indeed to be deliriously happy about the person you are—the very same person you have felt so ashamed of and rejected—opens the floodgates of acceptance for your children. Learning to love the seemingly unlovable parts of yourself enables you to embrace and care for the parts of your child that have been challenging for you. It's the basis of being able to love your children, your wider family, or indeed anyone in your life in an unconditional way.

The Rebirth of Feeling

When you dare to meet your own discomfort, then place it in the container of your compassion, you may experience an avalanche of feelings accompanied by tears. Tears can be so cleansing.

Beneath your discomfort, at the heart of the emotion, you will also experience a still, unapologetic, unprotected place that knows unequivocally just how precious you are. It's been waiting there all along. If you stay the course of your emotions long enough to meet and greet this place within you as it waits in quiet repose for you to come home to yourself, it will begin to transform your life.

What I've just described is the journey through our emotional birth canal. When we take this journey, it births us into our true identity. Joseph Campbell dubbed this "the hero's journey." Taken one emotional step at a time, it truly feels heroic. The new you that you birth yourself into is now yours by rite of consciousness. You earn it through your willingness to journey through the birth canal of your consciousness into your deep wisdom that has been waiting for you all along.

The conscious path for both individual and collective evolution embraces the messages our emotions seek to bring us. We are moving not so much toward the intensity of the emotion, but toward the unraveling of the energy caught up in reactivity, allowing it to be transformed into true feeling. The pain naturally dissipates once we receive the insight the message contains, and in its place love, joy, peace, and all the other deep states of feeling flood forth in service to our own evolution and then making this alchemized energy available for us to share with our children and the world. Our children sense the shift in us because transformation is palpable. Our own transformation provides liberation, not only in our own life, but liberation from the constricted energy in our relationships with our children and family.

The spark of true feelings of worthiness, inherent value, real joy and inspiration are ignited, not by by-passing pain, but by staying with the emotion long enough to receive the message that was seeking our attention and becoming reacquainted with our original, innocent being that has been waiting patiently to be reunited with us for so long. In this way, receiving the insight actually brings value to the pain.

Rather than avoiding pain and conflict with your children, seek to use the emotion they stir up to transform you. Allow it to awaken in you your true feeling self. As you do so, you will finally know that in the midst of your deepest pain, you are precious. Your children will learn from you, that in the midst of their own pain, they, too are precious.

12

Connection

" I felt like I had hit rock-bottom in my parenting with my daughter," Zara, a client, wrote. I imagine that you, too, have felt this way with your child at some point. I'd like to share with you how Zara handled it. In her letter to me, she related:

There was a lot of conflict between us, and I knew from working with you to look within myself. Because my irritation and anger with Sally were out of proportion to the situation, I realized so much of it was my stuff. Even though I was aware that this had to do with my own feelings of emotional abandonment as a child, when the going got tough between Sally and me, I would still act out. It was exceedingly painful, because I was trying so hard to be patient and understanding—all of the things I believed I wasn't. I left so many interactions between us feeling deeply remorseful.

The other evening at bedtime, Sally wanted to talk. I thought it was just a way for her to avoid having to go to bed, yet I also didn't want to shut her down. From the get go, we weren't connected. Trying to communicate seemed futile. When she said, "You use a mean tone with me too much," I became defensive. And when she began to use words like "always" and "every day" to describe how frequently I use a mean tone, I got triggered—especially since, for the last week, I felt I had been making progress in the way I spoke to her.

We were lying next to each other in her bed, with the lights out, when at one point she said, almost crying, "I just don't want this bad stuff between us."

I said, "It's okay. We always love each other. We're just trying to communicate better."

"How do I know you love me?" she asked.

I was taken aback by this and felt the nerve endings of blame and shame shoot up through my body, as I thought, "How have I failed as a parent that she could ask such a question?" Not really knowing how to answer her, I said, "Well, because of all the things I do for you to try to make your life better."

Through her tears, Sally said, "I just want a mom I can talk to. There are things I want to tell you, but when I do, you say 'Well, you should have done this or you shouldn't have done that,' instead of just saying, 'I get it.' "

I was blown away by how clear she was, and I stayed silent because I could find no words. Finally, I told her how moved I was by what she said, and that I "got it." I understood what she was trying to tell me. Thanking her for sharing how she felt, I explained that I was grateful she was able to articulate it so clearly.

It was then that I realized I had said, "You should know I love you by what I *do*," whereas she was saying, "I want to know you love me by how you can *be* with me."

What an epiphany! In that moment I felt my whole childhood flash before me. I had longed for that connection with my own mother. I wanted her to be authentic with me. I wanted to connect with her. I always felt she was only able to share a tiny bit of herself with me. I realized that my conflicts with Sally were a mirror of how disconnected I had been within myself.

When Zara and I talked, she expressed how important it had been for her to stick it out with Sally, painful though it had been to do so. Alongside gratitude for her ability to do this, she also felt enormous sadness over the way her parenting had led to so much strife. At one point Sally all but gave up on communicating what she wanted to say to her mother, muttering, «It won't matter anyway.»

Zara told me she felt like she needed to ask her daughter to be patient with *her*, because she realized she couldn't change the way she spoke to her overnight. She didn't want Sally to think their conversation had no lasting impact.

My next session with Zara helped her to articulate to Sally how important what she had said to her was and what an impact it had made on her. She let Sally know that she too wanted a deeply meaningful connection. Later Zara told me, "It was a profound moment of connection between us that was transformative for me as a parent."

Said this mother, "I began to see how my own inner disconnection was keeping me from simply being with my daughter. All she wanted was my presence and my understanding. She was able to express this so clearly, and I'm grateful I had sufficient awareness to be able to hear her."

One of the great insights in this story is that Sally so wanted to connect that *she moved toward her mother*, openly expressing how she experienced their relationship. If we could but realize it, our children *always* want to connect with us, even when they may appear to have shut down and are even quite hostile. Connection is the very fabric of life. Our children long for it, just as you may have longed for it—perhaps even silently, as so many children do.

How to Connect with Your Children

"Your task is not to seek for love," said Rumi, "but merely to seek and find all the barriers within yourself that you have built against it."

Connection is the cornerstone of life. This is especially so of relationships, particularly those with our children. We all want to feel seen, to feel valued, to know we matter. We yearn to belong and to feel cherished.

The poet Maya Angelou reminds us, "People will forget what you said, people will forget what you did, but people will never forget how you made them feel." So it is with our children. They will above all remember how we made them feel. When I ask my clients to remember back to their own childhood, they particularly recall wanting to feel seen, valued, and accepted.

Connection with our children flows from our connection with ourselves. Paradoxically, the more deeply we connect with our innermost being, the greater access we have to the whole of life.

I can't emphasize strongly enough that *acceptance of our children occurs only to the degree we accept ourselves.* We will treasure our children to the degree we treasure ourselves. It all starts within ourselves. Reconnect with yourself, and you will build strong bonds with your children.

It's so important to recognize that whenever we are triggered—when we are upset because our child is behaving a certain way—challenging as it may be, this has come into our life for the specific purpose of restoring our connection with our authentic self.

Can you recognize how, in your struggles with your child, life is supporting you in healing hurt from your own childhood, so that you can then experience a closer connection with your children? Children are part of nature's way of providing us with an opportunity to master life's curriculum, which is that we learn to live in a freer, more unencumbered manner that's peaceful, loving, and full of joy.

Children Can Help You Heal the Hurt of Your Own Childhood

There's a lovely practice of self-care that my clients often find truly fulfilling. Whenever you find yourself upset with your child, the first thing to do is recognize that it's a part of *yourself* that's upset. Some aspect of you didn't receive something you very much needed as a child, and now this is coming out toward your own child.

You're upset because an aspect of you didn't receive something that you, yourself, needed as a child. Now there are two children in the room. When you first provide for the hurting child within yourself, soothe yourself, you become able to provide for your child from a calm, centered, adult place able to be fully present for their needs. You must "grow yourself up" first, so to speak.

If you see *yourself* as hurt, needy, vulnerable, or self-conscious—a child in need, yourself—you are less likely to judge these feelings and more likely to experience empathy for them, knowing that these parts of you didn't receive the care they required in order to mature. Through this practice, you become your own nurturer, as you take responsibility for how you feel, how you speak, and how you behave.

When a children receive a scrape, such as by falling off a bicycle, we obviously put a bandaid on their injury. Yet what they often want most at such a time is our love and to feel connected to us. Well, it's no different in our own case. Any of the hurting places within us that didn't receive love are likely still looking for it.

The most beautiful definition of healing I have encountered comes from Drs. Ron and Mary Hulnick in their book *Loyalty to Your Soul,* where they write, "Healing is the application of loving to the place inside that hurts." The practice of offering your own loving self to the places within you that are hurting is, to me, simply exquisite.

One way to do this is to go to the mountaintop, look down, and ask any of the hurting places within you what they need—or, more accurately, what you needed way back when this would have helped soothe the aspect of you that's upset. What did you most need to hear back then? What did you need most? What would have made a difference for you? Listen with compassion. Listen with an open heart.

Once you hear what you most wanted to experience back then, you can provide this for yourself in the present. Perhaps you wanted to know that you weren't a burden, that you weren't to blame for your parents' turbulent relationship or maybe even their divorce, that you were a precious treasure who mattered to someone. Perhaps you longed to hear that you were "enough"—that you were okay just as you were, with nothing missing, nothing needing to be fixed.

Once you've identified what you longed for as a child, you can soothe yourself. The feeling of deep compassion with which you speak to yourself is at least as important, and perhaps even more important, than the actual words themselves. As Maya Angelou says, it's the *feeling* you give yourself that you'll most remember. Rock these hurting places within your own heart until the layers of protection melt into the container of compassion you have surrounded them with. You will find that beneath the shell of protection you built around yourself is a place deep within you that has always known you are enough. This is your childlike nature, which has long been waiting for your return to yourself.

When I speak of your "childlike nature," I'm not referring to the idea put forward a number of years ago concerning a "wounded inner child," which can quickly lead to feeling sorry for ourselves. This isn't about babying ourselves, handling ourselves with kid gloves, or catering to ourselves in a childish manner.

Dwelling on wounds from the past, going over and over them in our mind, has the effect of worsening the hurt, to the point that what happened to us can become our whole identity. We see ourselves as the "abused" person, the "victim." There's no healing in this. Going over and over something that happened to us, telling ourselves how awful it was—or talking endlessly about it with friends—only wears the grove deeper. We become like a well-rehearsed choir.

None of us is the child who experienced these things any longer. We are an adult who's feeling the effects. These effects need to be addressed compassionately in the way we weren't capable of as a child—a way that only an adult is capable of. We are no longer children, and any pain we experience left over from childhood needs to be addressed in the present as life brings it to our attention, such as through issues with our own children.

Our "childlike nature," is our original, core self—our authentic being, which is pure innocence. As Jesus said, unless we become like a little child again, we can't begin to experience the divine consciousness that, in the different language of that day, he referred to as the kingdom of heaven, which dwells within our own heart beneath all of our pain if we but connect with it.

Whenever you soothe yourself with your own compassion, the deeper "knowing" within you becomes courageous enough to surface. There's a place beneath the misperception of yourself that knows who you are and breathes a sigh of relief to be given life. When you untangle the knot of tangled thinking that has kept you from awareness of this "real" you, an inner expansion occurs. This inner spaciousness is the breath of authenticity that has been given life. It feels good to be in alignment with who you truly are.

All we have to be willing to do is express a sincere interest in the way we are hurting, along with the misperceptions we have acquired, then surround all of this with compassion. When we do, we won't need to reach for anything on the outside to try to find our own preciousness. Loving ourselves back to our original self is the only healing balm that can bring about an organic and lasting transformation.

You're Not a Screwup

This process is so beautifully illustrated by Barbara, a single mom to three teenage boys who came to work with me. Her oldest son, Jake had been drinking and was expelled from school. Although they tried quite a few times to talk about it, their attempts spiraled downhill, escalating to all-out yelling. Jake's behavior was so unacceptable to Barbara that she threatened to kick him out of the house if it ever happened again. Feeling unsupported, Jake flew out of the house in a rage, leaving Barbara distraught.

As I took Barbara up to the mountaintop to gain a more elevated perspective on her situation, she looked down and unexpectedly saw herself as a teen with her first boyfriend. She related how they really loved each other, but when she wanted to get more physical, he didn't. When he eventually broke up with her she was devastated, feeling rejected and alone.

At home her mother had called her fat (even though, looking back now, she realized she wasn't at all overweight). Consequently, she told herself that if she had been thinner, her boyfriend would surely have been interested in her physically. In her mind it was her fault he was no longer in her life.

Looking down from the mountain, Barbara saw a girl who believed herself to be "not enough"—and, as she described herself, "someone who would do anything to be accepted." In an instant, she not only felt compassion for herself, she also felt tremendous empathy for her son Jake. Just like her, he was trying to fit in at school and "would do anything to be accepted." He needed to believe he was okay even though he'd been expelled from school. He wanted to feel accepted despite having made a mistake. It was important for him to know he could screw up, but that he *himself* wasn't a screwup.

From the mountaintop, Barbara became her own nurturer. When she asked herself what she had most wanted to hear as a teenage girl, she heard a small voice respond, "I wanted to hear that *I* was okay even though my boyfriend broke up with me." Don't all of us long to know we are acceptable just as we are? Don't we yearn to know we aren't flawed?

Regardless of Jake's behavior, deep down all he wanted was to be accepted and connected to his mom. Over time, the two of them were able to talk about what they had learned about themselves through this incident. Ironically, because Barbara used the pain she experienced with respect to Jake's behavior to grow herself up, the result was that they were able to bond more deeply.

In my experience as a counselor, most of us have blurred the distinction between who we are and what we've done. We have forgotten the purity and innocence of our being and identify ourselves, instead, with our actions. When we do, our sense of ourselves stays on a roller coaster. When we behave "well," we feel good about ourselves and when we make mistakes, we think we are flawed. Yet, our being is distinct from our actions and we are all seeking to discern that who we are is precious and that we are all here to learn, grow and evolve.

When we discover our true nature as pure, we can accept ourselves even when we are learning hard lessons in life. This is such an empowering stance to pass on to our children. Imagine the acceptance your child feels when you accept them as precious and simply provide a container for their actions and behaviors.

Reclaiming the Gifts of the Mother

To commit to our own internal connectedness, living in a field of abundance, nourishing our own spirit, is the way to assure our children we can provide what they, like us, most long for. This is the beauty of self-care.

The advantage women have is that these are our natural gifts as mothers. We are inherently gifted connectors. We are in our element when we're relating. In part because of the additional thickness of the female corpus callossum—the connection between the two halves of the human brain—we are great at processing and truly being able to tune into other people. All of these qualities, which are paramount in creating the intimacy we all seek, are natural for us.

Accessing the ultimate energy, which is spiritual energy, enables us to feel fulfilled within ourselves. This allows us to utilize our natural wisdom and authority.

The tragedy is that many of us have abandoned our feminine giftedness—qualities such as feminine wisdom and insight. The miracle of bringing children into our life is that they provide us with an opportunity both individually and collectively to reclaim our ability to function in accordance with our nature.

Imagine the gift we give our daughters and sons when, through our reconnection to our orphaned self, they stay connected to their own childlike nature. Imagine the burden lifted from them when they are free to live out the life they truly came to live. They will have their own lessons to learn, but they won't be burdened with the added weight of our unlearned lessons. Liberated from our excess baggage, they will have an opportunity to be the beacons of authenticity we ourselves have yearned to be all along—and, through their impact on our life, are at last becoming.

It comes down to the fact that, in a very real sense, you are your own child. Raise yourself well.

13

The Field of Motherhood

"Out beyond ideas of right doing and wrong doing there is a field. I'll meet you there," wrote the mystic poet Rumi. As mothers, we spend so much of our time immersed in the physical, logistical tasks of family life, so much time in the world of diapers, meals, laundry, school life, homework, after school activities, cell phones, media, dating, driving, etc. It's so important for mothers to know ourselves to be of something higher—whole, perfect, more than enough, abundant—divine—allowing us to bring that higher energy into our daily life with our children. This is the field that our children already inhabit. This is what it means to be "in the world, but not of it." We must identify ourselves as something higher or we will succumb to a mundane experience of motherhood. When we are able to observe the world of duality, we can enter what the mystics speak of as the world of oneness.

As mothers it's so easy to see things as right or wrong, better or worse, good or bad. We think of ourselves as a good mom or a bad mom, happy or unhappy, rich or poor, a success or failure, having a good day or a bad day. We see our children's grades, behaviors, friends and accomplishments as acceptable or unacceptable. In other words, we tend to operate in an either-or mode of opposites, judgments, blame and shame.

Mothers want the best for our children, yet won't be able to fully hold the highest vision for them when we live mired in the world of right and wrong. Underneath the blame that most of us project onto our children and others, deep within us, we judge and blame ourselves for our mis-steps and mistakes. Judgment, blame and shame leaves us feeling separate and apart from our Essence and true self, like we are living anywhere but Rumi's infinite field.

Rumi invites us into a field that transcends our world of duality. Beyond ideas of right and wrong is the simple acceptance of "what-is." When we are able to be present with "what is", without the need to judge, blame or shame, we access the non-dual qualities of peace, love, joy, abundance, inspiration, patience, kindness and compassion available for us to inhabit.

This field Rumi speaks of exists beyond dualism. While the world operates in the either-or system of duality, this field—and the universe in which it manifests itself—operates in a both-and mode.

In this field of oneness, all things become possible.

Mother's Intuition

Shifting out of the paradigm of duality into a paradigm of oneness allows us to live a thoroughly human life with our children within a larger spiritual context. This is what it means to experience fulfillment.

We talked earlier about how, when most of us hear the word "spiritual," we tend to think of something different from our ordinary routine—something that only occasionally leaks into our everyday life. We saw that in actuality there is no discontinuity between our everyday human existence and what we are taught to think of as that "other" realm.

There is this world—made up of the things we can see, touch, taste, hear, and smell—and there is an infinite field of abundance in which all that we experience through our senses is happening. This field is so much vaster than the material things that make up a large part of our everyday existence, along with all of the thoughts and emotions we experience in reaction to what's happening around us. This infinite, unbounded field constantly infuses itself into that which we can see, touch, taste, and smell—and it's available to us anytime we open up to it.

Within this field is our mother's intuition. When we are simply present with "what is", we connect to the voice of wisdom within us that's always available to guide and direct our mothering. Every question about co-sleeping, vaccinations, cell phones, dating and media is answered from this field. We know ourselves and we know our children better than anyone else ever will.

I think you'll better understand what I'm trying to say when I tell you about my client Rebecca and her four-year-old-daughter, Leah. Rebecca described to me how Leah didn't want to get dressed to go to nursery school one morning. Because Rebecca works outside the home, she needed to be out of the house by a certain time. The more she tried to patiently reason with Leah, the more adamant Leah became, tossing down every outfit Rebecca offered her.

Whenever Rebecca begins to feel reactive, she has learned to turn her emotional energy away from her daughter, instead tuning into her own internal dialogue. When she did so that morning, she heard a panicked, fearful voice, frantically reminding her she was going to be late for work, late for a meeting, and likely to receive a reprimand from her employer. It was this that triggered the explosive energy she was feeling—energy that made her want to yell at her daughter to hurry up at all costs.

Rebecca saw two tantrums happening simultaneously, one in front of her and one within her. She could feel her heart pumping fast and her blood coursing through her veins. In the midst of her daughter's continued tirade, she began taking long, slow, deep breaths, soothing the panicked voice within her. Telling herself that it was understandable she was anxious, since she needed to get to work, she simply observed the dilemma she found herself in.

Rebecca told me that the turning point for her was when she realized she was doing the best she could in the situation and recognized her good intentions. Feeling "seen" and accepted in this way, she found herself relaxing somewhat. As she did so, she felt more peaceful inside. She even began to feel compassion for herself, as well as for her daughter. She realized they were two individuals who both simply wanted what was important to them.

As Rebecca began to feel connected first within herself, then to her daughter, she moved into a space of abundance.

Focusing her attention back on Leah she saw her daughter imitating the long, slow, deep breaths she herself had been taking, all the while continuing to toss her outfits down. It struck Rebecca that this was such a funny scene, and she found herself smiling compassionately at both of them.

In her expanded awareness, Rebecca was looking down at herself, perfectly at peace, even lighthearted. From this state of abundance, she realized that where before she had seen only two choices—Leah's way or her own—there were in fact other options for their morning, an entire field of possibilities.

Rebecca chose to let Leah just be where she was for the moment and went to finish gathering her things for work. By the time she returned to her daughter's room, she was able to calmly hold her boundary and peacefully guide Leah through the rest of her morning. Although Leah had been perplexed at first, as only moments ago her mother had been upset, she joined her mother in a full-on belly laugh. It was so liberating to laugh together at a situation that in the past would have remained so tense, probably locked into a power struggle with a "winner and loser" but neither of them happy.

Rebecca shared with me that one of her biggest awarenesses from this incident was an expanded concept of what self-care might look like. She had thought of it in terms of such things as lighting candles or taking bubble baths, which meant that at times it became one more thing on her to-do list, and therefore yet another task that felt burdensome. In contrast, it was something as simple as accepting and appreciating herself in her situation with Leah that reconnected her to herself and her abundant nature, providing her with exactly what she needed to shift her awareness.

Let's retrace the steps involved in this shift. When Rebecca first heard herself panicking and criticizing herself, she self-corrected, "No, but you are doing the best you can right now." Giving herself credit in this way made her feel seen and accepted. Talking to herself compassionately rather than in a critical manner took her from a constricted consciousness of lack to an expanded state of abundance. This self-nurturing created a bridge to a sense of inner connection and peace.

It wasn't until later when she was reflecting on her morning that Rebecca had the deeper realization that she had provided something for herself that had been missing when she was a young girl. She had never felt seen as a child. Now, viewing herself through compassionate eyes, she saw herself as a four-year-old who, just like her own daughter, had such strong ideas about what she had wanted to wear. Not only did Rebecca feel seen, but *she was able to see her daughter as well.*

Right in the midst of any challenge you are facing with your child, there is the potential for peace born of a sense of abundance. This peace, which is a characteristic of the field Rumi speaks of, is also available whether we are experiencing a difficulty with a coworker or a conflict with another country.

Let Your World Expand

Let's step back and take a wider view, that of Rumi's "field." We talked about how, in the world as most of us experience it, there's a duality of good or bad, winning or losing, success or failure. The world of duality is finite, limited, lacking. The field to which Rumi refers is infinite and abundant, full of possibilities and choices. When we enter into an awareness of this field, we sense an invisible yet infinite presence of which we are a part, and whose qualities—acceptance, love, joy, peace, abundance, wisdom, creativity, inspiration—are available to us at any moment.

In other words, when we expand our awareness, we realize that the infinite field of which I'm talking is larger than our present situation, and yet it contains our present situation. Whatever we may be going through—a conflict with our child, as was the case with Rebecca—it's contained within a larger, infinite reality that is always available to us if we but enter.

To get a handle on this, picture a child sitting on the floor in the cereal isle of a grocery store, fascinated by the different cartoon characters and colors on the cereal boxes. A few minutes later, the child looks up and, not seeing mom, becomes upset. To the child, she or he is all alone—a terrifying situation. What the child can't see is that mom is standing behind a display only a few feet away. Hearing her child's wails, she steps into view, and suddenly the child's entire perspective changes.

In a situation of this kind, all that has happened is that the child's world has expanded. They are seeing what they couldn't see before, which is that there was a nurturing presence there all along. This is exactly what happens to us when we become aware of the infinite field of conscious presence in which our lives are embedded.

To open our inner eyes in this way is exactly what it means to be "in the world" but "not of it." We are learning to live from the empowered state of the field that encompasses infinite potential, infinite possibilities. What this means is that we can experience what we are experiencing, and simultaneously be aware that our experience is part of a boundlessness, with limitless abundance, that's available to us at any moment. It isn't the opposite of anything—it's just a fuller picture.

In the middle of any situation with your child, practice stepping back and taking a larger view of the situation by your own simple acceptance of "what is." You'll find that there is an infinite presence inviting you to step into this expanded perception. Beyond the imaginary walls of your interaction there is a larger field—offering you peace, abundance, inspiration and compassion—in which to inhabit. This is the field of the mother.

To be spiritual—to be *holy*—is to be holistic, to recognize that we are whole and part of a whole. To be "spirit filled" is to live our daily life in the full consciousness that there are invisible qualities that are available to us, like the mother who was present for the child in the cereal aisle even when the child wasn't aware of her.

In this way, when our children come to us upset about something in their life—an unkind friend, a poor grade in school—you are able to inhabit the field of acceptance of "what is", your own portal to patience, kindness, agenda-less listening, compassion and connection for them. As you inhabit the field of the mother, you invite them into their own inner wisdom and essence—the field within them where all things are possible.

14

Make Friends with the Universe

Said Albert Einstein, the most important decision any of us will make during our lifetime is whether we believe we live in a friendly universe. What exactly did he mean, and what are the implications for our life as a mother?

To live a life fulfilled from the inside out, invites us to cultivate the knowing that we are supported by a friendly universe—that what is happening in our life is happening *for* us. In the midst of any circumstance we find ourselves in, there is some good seeking to emerge from that very situation. Children have this trusting relationship with the universe.

Our children come into the world utterly unable to do anything for themselves. Theirs is the ultimate in trust. While in the fragile state of infancy, they are dependent on us to meet their every need.

Children automatically *expect* each need to be supplied. It's entirely natural for them to assume they will be taken care of. It doesn't even occur to them that their needs will go unattended, as evidenced by the fact that they cry out for food when they are hungry and milk when they are thirsty. Their crying also lets us know when they are tired or in some other way distressed. They cry because they believe they will be heard and their needs will be met.

This was once your experience as well, and this innate sense of trust still lies deep within you. To reconnect with this trusting relationship with the universe is the key to working *with* life rather than feeling life is working against us.

Whereas we once saw the universe as benign, as we grow up and become more outwardly focused, we unknowingly confuse the benevolence and consistency of the universe with the inconsistency and duality of the world. We can slowly succumb to the mistaken belief that existence is arbitrary, uncaring, even punishing. This has a hugely negative effect on how a person functions. However, when we challenge this assumption about the nature of reality and make friends of the universe, our faith in the essential goodness of reality becomes a powerful force for good.

We all move through life experiencing situations through our own individual filters. Depending on our context, a situation will appear "positive" or "negative" to us. In reality, all situations are neutral. In and of themselves, they are neither good nor bad. It's our personal filter—our belief about something—that gives an event meaning. When we believe we live in a benevolent universe, we sense that all experiences are here to support our advancement.

Once we truly grasp this, we are inclined to focus less and less on whether the situation feels good or is pleasing, turning our attention more and more to how the particular circumstance we may be experiencing right now—especially with our children—is here to assist our development. Rather than labeling situations as good or bad, we look beneath the situation itself for the "good" that is seeking to emerge.

We begin to understand that for the universe to be friendly doesn't mean everything always feels good. "Friendly" means that everything is here to help us grow toward our potential, which is held in escrow within us, waiting to be realized.

This is especially important where life with our children is concerned. It is so easy to see situations and circumstances with our children as "against" us, not for us or simply negative. This leaves us feeling fearful and like a victim.

However, when we observe situations as happening for our good—for our evolution toward a more fulfilling life—we discover an infinite presence that at all times supports us and is here for us to lean into.

The universe is benevolent not because everything we experience feels good, but because everything is in service to our highest good. Everything we experience is here to further our growth.

How Your Child Invites You to Grow

To see how life is using situations to invite us to grow can be challenging at first, especially in our relationship with our children. When we have daughters or sons, unresolved issues from our past become magnified. Although you might not think so, this is a *good* thing.

The universe has a way of catching our attention so that it can assist us in resolving longstanding issues that have obstructed our ability to live our life to the fullest. A facet of our unconsciousness gets ushered into the light of conscious awareness so that we can address it and find the gem in our own inner rough. Once we come to completion on the matter, we are more able to live the life we came her to live, free and unencumbered.

Suppose that, before having a child, you cared far too much about what other people thought of you. Now that you have a child, if you allow your concern about what others think of you to persist, anytime your child acts out, you're going to worry *all the more* about other people's opinions. You'll likely find yourself asking, "What kind of mother will they think I am?"

Whether you see your reaction as a negative thing to be avoided, or as a beneficial thing that's actually assisting you in your growth, will determine whether you move to the next stage of your development.

If you see your reaction as a negative thing, you'll likely seek to control your child's behavior, in the hope that people will think highly of you. If you relate to your child's behavior as something with the potential to support your own growth, you'll see it as an opportunity to resolve your issue of being overly concerned about what others think of you. In this case, *your child just became part of the solution rather than a problem to be fixed.*

When your child acts out, have you ever thought of turning your attention away from the behavior for a moment, and even away from what you imagine others will think of you?

When we shift our attention to our own inner discomfort instead of focusing on our child's behavior, we give ourselves an opportunity to comfort the place within us that has been externally focused and therefore concerned about what others think. We recognize that our feelings have arisen because there's discontent and unrest within us that requires soothing and completion.

Once we arrive at this realization, what to do?

Simply soothing ourselves with compassion from the mountaintop takes care of the issue. We turn toward our own inner discontent and away from our child's behavior. Whenever we calm *ourselves* rather than reprimanding our child, we discover that by soothing the uncomfortable places within us, we are able to remain calmer the next time our child acts out.

Paradoxically, as we learn to calm ourselves, over time this has a calming effect on our child. Additionally, it models for our children how to soothe themselves without the need to reach for something from the outside like drugs, alcohol, shopping or sugar.

Do you see how two people can have two entirely different experiences when their child acts out? One sees it as a problem to be fixed, whereas the other sees it as an opportunity to heal a wound that is opening within themselves. It's all a question of whether you believe that everything is here to further our growth.

How It Works in Real Life

To illustrate from the case of a client of mine in her early forties, Jane desperately wanted to have a child. Having experienced three miscarriages, she subsequently sought help from the best fertility clinics in the country. At times unable to become pregnant, and at other times unable to carry a child to term, the best technology ultimately failed to help her.

Throughout her journey, Jane was strangely drawn to the idea that the universe is benevolent, though she found herself struggling to believe it because of her experience. What was she to make of her inability to conceive and carry a child to term? It certainly didn't look like the universe was supporting her in her most important dream. She began asking what good was seeking to come from this situation, what she was here to learn, how she was here to grow.

Deciding to leave her job in Tennessee, Jane and her husband relocated to San Francisco, where Jane had taken a higher-paying position. It was as if she was trading her dream of a child for a dream of a better job. Deeper within her, though, something was prompting her to let go of the tight control she was placing on getting pregnant and the tight control that permeated her relationships and decisions in her life. Although getting pregnant was so important to her, she followed her inner promptings to relax and let go a little. The move was intended to give them a fresh start, which included taking some time away from trying to have a child, along with focusing on other aspects of their lives.

When Jane finally visited a doctor in the San Francisco area, he was more interested in her stress levels and restoring a sense of balance to her life than her age or lab reports. When he explained that sometimes a more Zen approach was often better than the methods she had been trying for so long, Jane listened. Within weeks, with minimal medical intervention, she was expecting. Nine months later she was mom to a beautiful girl.

For Jane and the fertility clinics she had at first frequented, it had all been about how low the odds were for a woman of her age to conceive.

The San Francisco doctor's response was that there was no reason she couldn't "get lucky." Proposing a light dose of medication, rather than the bazooka of drugs she had been subjected to previously, the San Francisco doctor commented, "Sometimes you just have to zen your way to these eggs." His approach reflected the less controlled manner she had been prompted to take in her own life.

The reason I mention Jane's situation isn't so much because she ultimately became pregnant, which is quite the miracle. The reality is, this doesn't happen for everyone—for reasons we'll talk about in a moment. But what *can* happen for all of us is that, like Jane, we choose to move through every experience in our life in a manner that's true to our inner being. Jane followed the guidance of her inner wisdom recognizing the need to release the tight, controlling way she was living. She was learning to let go.

Jane was learning to create a trusting relationship with the universe, rather than succumbing to the seemingly negative situation she had been enduring, Jane had the courage to follow her intuition to change location. Of course, she imagined she was moving for a job. She didn't realize she was being guided to a particular doctor who would assist her in becoming pregnant easily and naturally.

Einstein was insightful when he said we make a pivotal choice when we decide whether the universe is friendly or hostile—whether we live in a supportive reality that's not only capable of providing for our needs, but that's infinite in its resources and consequently infinitely giving.

Is Life Really Meant to Be "Comfortable"?

Especially through the media, we are taught that we are here to feel good and be comfortable. We are bombarded with endless temptation to seek a comfortable life. A comfortable home, a comfortable job, a comfortable car, a comfortable chair, a comfortable bed—these and other material comforts are supposed to make our life satisfying. As well, we are comfortable when our children behave in a manner we find acceptable, receive certain grades and accolades. We're taught to base our sense of ourselves on their behaviors.

When we base our sense of security on material things, the result is that our life becomes a roller coaster, whereby whether we feel comfortable or uncomfortable at any given moment depends on our circumstances. It's a roller coaster because the physical world is constantly changing and therefore can only ever bring us a temporary experience of comfort, safety, and security. Do you see how, when we look to the material world, our peace is always going to be fleeting at best?

Because we like to think that life is meant to be comfortable, when something distressing happens our first reaction is, "Why is this happening to me?" It may surprise you to hear that our "why" isn't a plea for understanding of the reason something is occurring, but a cry of protest. Even if we were given accurate information about the circumstances we find ourselves in, it still wouldn't satisfy the underlying feeling that "this shouldn't be happening."

In contrast, when we turn our attention inward, seeking comfort from our essence, we discover a wellspring that provides us with a fulfillment and a contentment that our material existence can't begin to give us. We find ourselves liberated from the emotional roller coaster of life's constant ups and downs.

Do you see how just because something isn't comfortable or our child acts out, doesn't mean it isn't working for our good and theirs? Just because Jane's situation was extremely uncomfortable didn't mean that it wasn't serving a valuable purpose in her life. She and her husband grieved together, from which she learned to relax and trust the process of life—something that had always been a struggle for her. As she did so, she trusted her way right into having the child she had always dreamed about. Even had she not become pregnant, she and her husband learned to find fulfillment within themselves and with each other. They had thought about adoption and may still choose to adopt because of this experience.

One of the biggest myths many of us buy into is the idea that life is meant to feel good and be a comfortable experience. At the same time, the fact that life isn't always going to be comfortable in no way contradicts what we have said about the benign nature of the universe. On the contrary, it's often through the discomfort we experience that we at last open up to the reality that the universe intends to provide for our maximum fulfillment.

While we may gravitate toward comfort, the reality is that our inner being is perfectly content to experience life in *all* its manifestations, ranging from the bliss and ecstasy of unconditional love to the grief that follows the loss of a love. This is the experience the human soul signs up for. As we release the need for life to feel good, especially where life with our children is concerned, we increasingly experience the richness and fullness it has to offer on all fronts.

In this, we can learn from our children, who don't have a need to feel comfortable all the time. When a child is learning to walk, they stand up, topple over, stand up again, fall headlong—over and over. Their goal isn't to feel comfortable, but to walk, and they are willing to persevere through the discomfort of falling again and again in order to reach this next stage of their development. They are internally oriented, connected to something within themselves that compels them to keep going. The discomfort is part of the journey. They are okay when the process is uncomfortable. It isn't to be avoided.

One advantage of embracing this insight is that we no longer feel a need to push anything away from us. We don't cling to some experiences, while fighting off others. On the contrary, our mindset becomes one of "everything is here to support my growth." Far from being something to avoid, the experiences that appear to cast a shadow over our path are to be drunk from, learned from, and incorporated into a life well lived.

The universe is a neutral environment replete with impersonal laws that operate consistently. Life functions like a mirror, reflecting back to us our own degree of awareness. It does so for the sole purpose of our conscious transformation. Like our children learning to walk, when our journey isn't comfortable, we can learn to see it as life supporting us in reaching for our potential.

The universe sees the darkness and the light the same way—as opportunities for your soul to evolve. It exists to supports this mandate. The paradox is, when you stop resisting the discomfort, it oddly becomes a rich experience, full of depth and a connection that transports you to a world where your soul abides and mysteriously understands.

15

From Ego to Essence

Think back to meeting your child, or children, for the first time. Or perhaps a moment of being present with a newborn or young child. How did it feel? When my son was born, it was an awe-inspiring experience. Simply being in my child's presence made me aware of a life beyond the ordinary. In his undefended "being" state, he transported me into a world beyond this one.

If we allow ourselves to be truly present with a newborn or young child, we get to witness a human being in the natural state. If we allow it to—if we are sufficiently aware—it will reverberate with our *own* natural state, which I have been referring to as our "essence." This is the awakened state we're seeking to inhabit while living our life each day, and especially in our relationship with our children.

In any moment of your day today, no matter how distant you may feel from your authentic self, you need only become present again with the experience of meeting your child for the first time and you'll likely find yourself effortlessly reconnecting with your own essential being.

I encourage clients to keep pictures of both themselves and their own children as infants quite visible throughout the home. Often mothers create a special area in their bedroom or office with a few precious photos that evoke a feeling of the pure potentiality within this undefended child. When we look back at ourselves or our children during infancy or during those first few years of life, we become aware of an innocence that can sometimes go unnoticed in our everyday life, yet is still there in potential. When that undefended innocence is ignited within us, our very vibration is raised and we are connected to a presence that is larger than our life.

This can also occur when we take the time to simply look into our child's eyes, no matter their age—or our own, for that matter. I often suggest to my clients to watch their children sleeping because it does something to the *parent,* transporting them back to their own essential nature and the infinite, unbounded nature of life. The more we practice this, the more we relate to our children from this place in our day-to-day life. It becomes the norm rather than the exception.

I often have clients keep a photo of themselves or their child as an infant next to their bed and take the time each morning or evening to look at that photo for three minutes. I have never had a mother look at themselves or their child's photo for a solid three minutes without having something shift in their body and their perception. Their heart opens and expands, and they experience a deep connection within themselves. Sometimes there are tears of loss, regret, sadness, grief, longing, and yearning—but also of reconnection. Tears are cleansing. Behind those tears is our yearning for connection. Stay with the tears, and you find your true self.

On a practical note, many parents find bedtime a challenging time in their relationship with their children. We are exhausted with nothing left to give to our child. Our tank is empty. Yet at the very time when we are spent from the day, our children need connection the most.

When I look deeper at this phenomenon with parents, I realize that it's the parent needing their own inner connection that "me" time provides. It's the parent who has become disconnected from themselves.

When parents choose to look at a photo of themselves as a child, or simply look into their child's eyes with the intention of connecting inwardly with themselves, they connect with their own preciousness as a child—and simultaneously, with the preciousness of their own child.

My client Yuki shared with me a bedtime routine she created for herself and her son Hiroshi. She explained:

I used to dread bedtime. I was exhausted, and no matter what I did or said, or how long I stayed with Hiroshi, he wanted more of me. Almost every night ended in stress and tears. I knew something needed to change, so I made it a self-care challenge for myself.

I found a picture of Hiroshi sleeping, and I placed it in a beautiful frame next to his bed. That night, we each held the photo. I looked at the photo of my son sleeping so peacefully, then began speaking about *myself*. "Yuki," I said, "You have had a wonderful day. You experienced many things. You talked with many people and made many decisions. You had special time with Hiroshi at the park. You cooked a beautiful dinner for your family. You are with your beautiful son right now. You are ready for sleep after a long day."

Then I turned to Hiroshi and began speaking to him. "Hiroshi, you did many things as well today. I'm so grateful I got to pick you up after school. I'm grateful we got to spend special time at the park together. I'm grateful I got to have dinner with you. I'm grateful I got to give you a bath. I'm grateful I get to tuck you in. I'm especially grateful I get to be your mommy. I am the luckiest mommy on earth."

Because I had found a way to authentically put myself into the nighttime equation, this turned into such a rich and connected time for us. Simply acknowledging my own long day and stating aloud that I'm tired and ready for sleep soothed me. I accepted myself as tired, and it moved me into a spaciousness that I hadn't experienced at bedtime. From this place, I was able to listen patiently and be sincerely interested as Hiroshi talked about his day and what was important to him.

When we connect with our own preciousness, it takes us out of the daily bedtime routine—the day-to-day doing—and into a state of *being* that's larger than our own life. We can experience how fleeting our time on earth is. We experience how grateful we are for our life and the life of our child. We can reconnect to what's really important. We fill up our own tank, and our children feel the shift. Our very presence soothes them.

Because children live so fully in their essence, they have the power to reconnect us to our own. To be connected to our essential nature is the true definition of fulfillment. Whether you are a CEO, a celebrity, a clerk in an office, a factory worker, or a waiter or waitress—whether you are single or partnered—in your deepest self, you yearn to live a fulfilling life. Children, by their very *being*, can show us how to reconnect with our ability to live our life full out.

Because our children naturally inhabit what I often refer to as their "being space," they still live in their essence. Consequently, as Kahlil Gibran says, instead of seeking to have them become like us, it's we who need to embody the essence state they now occupy. In this way, we come back home to our authentic self.

We tend to think we need to wait until some pristine moment to enter into our essence, but the opposite is true. It's precisely in the midst of our everyday life that entering into our essence is both possible and powerful.

Children demonstrate this to us so clearly. When children play, they are operating in their natural state, which is one of abundance. They don't think of all the obstacles, problems, or limitations of a situation. Rather, they are simply their essential self—free, unencumbered, and present in the moment.

Children "work" when they play. They dig up dirt, dump it into a wheelbarrow, and deliver it to the other side of the backyard—all with such complete abandon and joy. Children are serious about their play! Their work is their play, and their play is their work—there's no distinction between the two. Their *doing* flows from their *being*, so that it's all the same to them. They are invested and immersed in being and doing at the same instant.

Instead of training our children away from their natural state, we can learn to parent from *our* essence. To parent from my essence, which has a feel of abundance, flow, and "world without end," is my highest aspiration as a mother.

Your Ego is Your Friend

Earlier, we explored a wonderful statement by Rumi concerning meeting in the field. Now I'd like us to examine a poem of his in which our human ego can be likened to visitors in a guest house, the guest house being our essence. In The Guest House, he writes:

This being human is a guest house.

Every morning a new arrival.

A joy, a depression, a meanness,

some momentary awareness comes

as an unexpected visitor.

Welcome and entertain them all!

Even if they are a crowd of sorrows,

who violently sweep your house

empty of its furniture,

still, treat each guest honorably.

He may be clearing you out

for some new delight.

The dark thought, the shame, the malice,

meet them at the door laughing and invite them in.

Be grateful for whatever comes,

because each has been sent

as a guide from beyond.

We tend to think that it's hard to live from our essence, the guest house, because of our ego. Consequently, we tell ourselves we need to banish our ego—those guests we deem unattractive—in order to reside in our essence. If you think about this, it implies that the ego is the "big" thing in our life, whereas our essence is rather small and difficult to find, let alone enter into and live from.

This may surprise you, especially with so much talk about the ego these days, but the reverse is actually more accurate. Our essence is infinite—so vast, in fact, that it actually *contains* our ego.

If you see this once about yourself, I can't tell you how liberating it will be. Once you realize that your essence envelopes your ego, and you'll give up the struggle to "get rid of" your ego. In fact, the more you befriend all the guests in the house of your essence, the more peaceful and joyful you will become. More and more, you'll find yourself living from your essence.

Isn't this what we all wanted from our own parents? Didn't we simply want all of ourselves to be accepted and embraced? Didn't we want to be fully seen and accepted, warts and all?

Why is this relevant to our lives as mothers? When we practice accepting all parts of ourselves—especially those parts that we call the ego and tend to disown, judge and cast away—we teach our children that all parts of themselves are acceptable of love. When we learn to accept all aspects of ourselves, we are also more able to embrace all aspects of our children. This profound practice of self-acceptance is undervalued. When we fully accept the dark, shadowy places within ourselves, we automatically become accepting of our children and all those around us.

It's not an exaggeration to say that wars will end when full self-acceptance begins.

This is why I am so certain that mothers are here to change the world. We have the capacity to embrace the shadow. Mother Teresa was able to embrace those perceived to be the fringes of society. When we embrace our own inner fringes, we become a powerful force of change within our families, society and the world-at-large.

Much has been written about the ego over the ages, going back thousands of years in fact. The term has actually changed meaning over the course of time and is sometimes used to refer to quite different elements of our humanity. Especially recently, the ego seems to get a bad rap.

The way I use the term ego, it's most simplistically defined as the way we identify ourselves—the way we imagine ourselves to be, think of ourselves, picture ourselves in our mind. Our ego is the survival mechanism we formed in order to navigate situations we encountered in which we felt threatened. Understood this way, the ego consists of layer upon layer of armor, used to defend us from potential hurt from the world around us.

I love the phrase, "Hindsight is 20-20." There is such value in looking back, not in regret or with judgment, but to learn from my past in order to enrich our lives. Today I recognize that at the time my ego developed, I was doing the best I could within my own particular circumstances. At the time, developing an ego as a means of protecting myself was my best, though ultimately unsuccessful, attempt to care for myself.

Once formed, we naturally carry our childhood defenses into adult life, where they are simply frozen and now tend to act against our best interests. These aspects of ourselves whose growth has become stunted require our conscious assistance in order to mature. In other words, we need to accept the ego and embrace it with compassion, not fight it. It is our ego that is calling out to be seen for what it is trying to do for us. It is our ego that is calling out to feel connected. Once we connect to our ego in compassion and love and see it for what it is seeking to do for us, the protective layers melt away.

As Katy Carlson, a wise mother-friend of mine used to say, "The sun doesn't concern itself with the density of the shadow, the sun only concerns itself with the giving of its light." Our essence is not concerned with the density of the ego. Our essence is concerned only with bathing the ego in its light. It is in this light that the ego will feel met and consequently, effortlessly and gracefully melt into the ocean that is our essence. We will find all of our inner aspects flowing in the same direction and our life becomes a mighty river flowing in the direction of our destiny.

How ironic that, years later as adults, *we tend to castigate those same egoic layers we developed to protect us from the external world.* Paradoxically, when we accept every part of ourselves instead of battling with ourselves—when we simply become aware of the egoic aspects of ourselves and contain them in our own compassion—little by little the protective shell of our ego dissolves and we find ourselves back in the essential "feel" of ourselves that a child inhabits.

Befriend Your Ego

In *The Guest House*, Rumi highlights the importance of not pitting ego against essence. Instead, he suggests we welcome the different aspects of our ego, our various house guests—that we invite them in and treat them honorably, thanking them for what they have to teach us. This is a fundamentally different approach from the judgmental stance so many of us have learned to take toward our ego—a stance that has us living in a house divided.

I judged my ego for a long while, believing it kept me away from my essence. But all I did was strengthen it. Now, instead of judging my ego, which leads to constantly being at war with it, I have come to see the innocent intention of the ego. As I look back on my childhood from the mountaintop, I find myself not wanting to struggle against my ego, but instead to observe it through the eyes of compassion.

The truth is that our ego has actually been in service to our essence. This is beautifully described by one of my clients, Samantha, who related her experience of at last embracing her ego while in counseling with me:

As a young child who had been molested but told no one about it, I desperately wanted connection. Yet at the same time the last thing I wanted was for you to know me, really know me. Instead I wanted to appear perfect. I wanted to be acknowledged but not known.

I was so consumed with hiding that I couldn't let you in. I learned how to size you up, figure out what you needed me to be, then "be her" for you. In other words, since I believed you wouldn't really accept me, I created a "me" I thought you could more easily accept. It was such an investment of time and energy, inviting you in close enough that I could feel some semblance of the connection I so longed for, then pushing you away so you wouldn't really see me. It was a push-pull of loneliness really.

To push you away, I needed to make you wrong. I felt so "wrong" inside myself that I felt you would certainly reject me, which is why I needed to reject you first. I felt ashamed of who I thought myself to be deep down. My wall of protection was so thick that no one was able to pierce through. I had created a double bind for myself—wanting intimacy, yet pushing it away at all costs. As an adult, I judged myself harshly for this. How could such an intelligent, loving woman fail so miserably at relationships, especially with my own children?

All I want is a close relationship with them. I find myself feeling close and then in an instant, I'll do or say something that pushes them away. I'll complain or judge or find something wrong and then feel so remorseful and deeply alone and disconnected from the very beings I long to connect with.

It was on the mountaintop, looking down at my life and my struggles, that the severe judgement I'd dealt myself first began to melt. It began to make perfect sense to me that if I thought myself to be damaged goods, I'd naturally want to protect you from seeing me. I began to understand how my ego had sought to help me. I began to see my ego through the eyes of compassion rather than judgment. Why would I condemn a part of myself that had been struggling to keep me safe?

From the mountaintop, I realized that judging my ego was keeping my survival system intact. At the same time, I saw how my judgment of these layers of protection, each established for my safety, were causing me to feel separate and very alone. I was running from you and I was running from me.

There on the mountaintop, I finally felt compelled, after years of abuse, to run *toward* my ego with my compassionate heart, rather than away from it in judgment. As I acknowledged the part of me that was trying to save me from additional pain and heartache, I began to give *myself* the love I so desperately wanted from the outside. I allowed myself to enter into those places within myself that had either withered or hardened, nurturing them with self-compassion.

I learned to see and connect to the very place inside of me that so desperately wanted love. I learned to reassure that place that I was okay and lovable. It's like I started singing love songs to the place within me that so wanted someone to sing to her. Who knew it would be so powerful to sing myself a love song!

I had lived as a traumatized child, but now my own self-soothing increasingly settled me down. As I gradually relaxed within myself, it felt safe to show you more of me. This was because, little by little, *I* was accepting more of me—the parts that had been abused and the parts that covered up that abuse. Eventually there was no part of me I needed to hide. I was at last experiencing the feeling of inner transparency I had always yearned for but never thought possible for someone like me.

I've heard it said that intimacy means "into me I see." From the mountaintop, I was able to see into all of myself with eyes of compassion and acceptance. I am in a healthy, mutually caring relationship for the first time in my life. The relationship with my children is equally as connected. They can tell me anything now. They can come to me about anything. I am a safe haven for them. I never imagined it would come by accepting the darkest, most hidden places within myself.

Samantha speaks for so many of us as we judge and push away from us the very places within us that need our love the most. I realize that many teachers condemn the ego thinking that it is the ego that seeks to keep us separate. But I have found that when we befriend it instead, simply accepting ourselves warts and all, we find ourselves melting into our essence—our most natural self, which has been at our center all along. We find this essence to be so expansive that there's no need to push away any part of ourselves. Our spirit knows it needs to fight against nothing. When we stop fighting, everything gradually and effortlessly melts into the intrinsic goodness of our being.

Our Children as Visitors in the Guest House

Our children give us the gift of helping us come back home to ourselves. This is because the relationship we need to have with ourselves is identical to the relationship we need to foster with them.

Just as we are learning to accept every part of ourselves, we are also learning to fully accept our children in the many different forms they show up. With our children, we never know what to expect. As Rumi says, they sometimes show up as "the joy, the meanness, or sometimes a crowd of sorrows, who violently sweep your house empty of its furniture." As mothers, we are our children's guest house, here to hold their joy as well as their crowd of sorrows violently sweeping our house empty of its furniture! So too with our own consciousness. The more able we are to befriend our own internal visitors—our own crowd of sorrows—the more smoothly our inner household will run. We find ourselves more and more able to embrace our children with all their many different aspects.

In *The Seat of the Soul*, Gary Zukav writes, "When the personality comes fully to serve the energy of its soul, that is authentic empowerment."

Essence is an awakened state of *being*, in which we are present to "what is" without judgment or commentary. We see this when we observe young children. They live in their essence, and their work and their play seem to serve a higher purpose.

The ultimate question in any moment becomes, "Am I living from my essence or from my ego? Am I parenting from my essence or ego? Am I seeing through the filter of abundance or fear, wholeness or lack?"

16

Self-Care as a Spiritual Practice

Life can feel quite mundane, or it can feel exalted. Self-care is a form of spiritual practice that's intended to infuse an expansive state of being into our ordinary everyday experiences. There's a sense in which it connects us with a world beyond our world.

When I use words like "exalted" or speak of an "expansive state," I'm not talking about deserting our ordinary routine in order to go find something out of the ordinary. Rather, it's about connecting with the extraordinary that's already present in our everyday experience. For instance, have you ever stopped to notice how a glorious, even sublime energy is everywhere present?

I'm talking about the feeling that often arises when we are out in nature. We might be gazing up at a sunset, walking in a forest, strolling through a meadow, or be by the ocean. This same feeling is there when we marvel at the utter perfection of a rose, experience the magic of romantic love, or look up at the galaxies in an infinite night sky.

For me, listening to a piece of music or gazing into the eyes of someone I love can take me into the feeling I'm referring to. In an instant, I enter a world that contains my everyday life and yet is boundless and transcends my limited world. I haven't "gone" anywhere, and yet I'm transported into a reality that's resplendent—a reality that, had I only noticed, was there all along. I have awakened to a beauty that can't be quantified, and yet is recognized by the heart. The energy that feeds the trees and clouds, and even breathes our breath, is an inexhaustible source that pours forth creative energy in every moment.

In the past, spirituality has tended to be separated from our everyday world as if it somehow weren't part of an ordinary lifestyle. Today, more and more of us understand spiritual practice as a tool for becoming aware of the sacred nature of *everything*, then living an extraordinary life in the most ordinary of ways. It's about treating everyone and everything we do as sacred, which means with dignity, kindness, and respect. As we bring an awareness of the sacredness of everything into our everyday world, we make our spirituality the heart of our lifestyle and are able to bring this way of being into our life with our children.

In other words, spiritual practice goes beyond merely blurring the lines between the sacred and the secular. In fact, it shows us that they are one and the same. The extraordinary mystery of life informs our everyday relationship with our children and infuses our ordinary activities with them, so that they become indistinguishable. The beauty of this is that it doesn't depend on our personal religious orientation, or whether we have a religion at all.

Where to Find the Energy You Long For

I heard a story about a three-year-old child who had just become a big brother. As he approached the newborn's crib, his mother overheard him say to his baby brother, "Please tell me again what it's like where you came from. I'm beginning to forget."

This story is relevant to all mothers. The connection we experience with our children when we meet them—the sense of our fundamental oneness—is undeniable. Yet how quickly we forget this when a baby is crying because of colic or wakes us up just after we got back to sleep following a feeding or diaper change.

Cherie, a new mother with a seven-month-old little girl, shared with me how she and her husband intended to stay in touch with the sacred energy they felt through their connection with their newborn. "And yet, even in the short time Malika has been in our lives," Cherie confided, "it's so easy for my husband and me to become caught up in the daily routine of laundry, preparing baby food, or getting Malika in and out of her car seat, that we forget the larger reality of our intrinsic oneness that was so apparent to us both at her birth and during those first few precious weeks of her life."

Cherie was right—it is indeed easy to forget, which is why we need an anchor to keep us centered on what's truly important. Self-care is this anchor.

When I talk about self-care, I'm not just referring to things like a manicure—although it can certainly take this form. I'm speaking about an energy that nourishes us in a way that sustains us and that can only be experienced on the spiritual level. This energy, which flows from a higher level of consciousness than many of us are accustomed to, is what makes things like manicures *more than just a manicure,* so that we experience them as a way of manifesting the fulfillment we already enjoy in our essence. They become a material channel for an immaterial way of *being.*

We all have the ability to tap into this inexhaustible energy simply by engaging in a little self-care. When we do so, it becomes the source of a whole new approach to motherhood—which involves living from a state of *overflow* instead of depletion. The irony is that the spiritual practice of inner-care is the very thing that so many of us "don't have time for."

If I had to choose only one thing that has the potential to change our current model of motherhood, it would be inner-care. So, as a mother, are you ready to cultivate the courage to take "me time," and to do so guilt-free? Can you recognize the value it brings?

You Are Here to Shine

Renee is raising a special needs child, Karen. Allow me to share with you how she describes her journey:

As mothers, we are naturally focused on the developmental milestones and growth of our children. Furthermore, as special needs moms, we are constantly testing and monitoring our children to see how they measure up to others of the same age. We also want to know how they are faring based on their last assessment. All these comparisons and testings can be so stressful and exhausting.

What a process it is to accept the child that has been given us in all of their forms. How could I accept my precious Karen in all of the different ways she shows up in a given day, when I was challenged and feeling so overly responsible for her every success or stumble?

I had a life-changing epiphany and a huge "aha" moment during Karen's second year in kindergarten. I had made the decision to be a stay-at-home mom because it was a financial possibility for me and, having been raised by a stay-at-home mom myself, it was something I always assumed I would do.

As you know, raising a special needs child can entail so many, many years of developmental therapies, evaluations, and testing. When one of Karen's therapists was responding to my excitement about a recent neuro-psych evaluation, the doctor said to us, "The sky is the limit for Karen." I was so proud and beaming that the sky was the limit for my special needs daughter.

Then the doctor turned to *me* and said, "And Renee, the sky is the limit for you as well."

What a life-changing moment for me! It was so believable for me to hear that Karen could do whatever *she* wanted in life. And yet, until that moment, I had never considered that this was also possible for myself.

What liberation I have experienced as I've nurtured the hurting places within myself. I knew there was a level of stress and anxiety within me, but I was struggling just to power through each day to meet Karen's needs. I had no idea that nourishing my own spirit would create such a welcoming place for my sweet Karen to land.

As we're on this journey of making sure our children are able to develop into these bright and shining souls, our own stars can simultaneously tend to dim. When I heard the doctor say that the sky is the limit for my life as well as my daughter's, he was giving me a permission I was ready to receive. I felt an elation within me—a knowing that this was possible for me all along. We are *both* here to be shining souls.

A spiritual practice is both restorative and simultaneously a process of awakening. We are awakening to and restoring within us what already *is*. We're not trying to get to someplace else, but waking up to what's already here, both within us and around us. Spiritual teacher Michael Bernard Beckwith, from whom I've learned so much, describes this as "opening our inner eyes to see the invisible and hear the inaudible."

Nourishing our spirit, nourishing our inner-life is a portal to this sublime realm that permeates the different areas of our daily life, especially our relationship with our children. I believe self-care to be essential to parenting in a conscious manner. It's so powerful for your child to see you taking good care of yourself.

Once we give ourselves permission to enter this expansive way of being, we draw to ourselves situations that reflect this more relaxed and connected way of life. When we are connected to the state of abundance, we experience possibility rather than lack—yes, even amid the challenges that come with parenting.

The sad fact is that many mothers, earnestly trying to parent in a more conscious way, are attempting to do so from an empty tank. In contrast, when we nourish our spirit and our inner-life, not only does our life flourish but we have more to give to our children. We are able to be present and available to their inner-needs. Self-care, with it's mutually beneficial effect, becomes a way of life.

Self-Care as a Way of Life

If you begin to experience the feeling of well-being that comes from self-care, you won't want to go a day without it. Self-care becomes a way of life, a habit like brushing your teeth. You take care of yourself not only for yourself but so that you can also better serve those around you—your spouse, children, wider family, friends, co-workers and your community.

In order for self-care to become a way of life it must be something that fits easily into your schedule in a complementary way. In my case I live near a park, so walking is a perfect fit for me. I'm also a musician and appreciate music, so music fills my soul. Both of these activities are easy for me to include in my daily routine and don't require a lot of extra effort. Perhaps you are a painter, or maybe you love gardening, art, animals, or cherish time with friends. Whatever you choose, let it be something that nourishes your inner-life and spirit.

Once you find things that fit easily into your day, you'll be amazed by how inspired you become. This inspiration will bring more joy, creativity, and love into your life than you can imagine. You'll have to stretch to receive the waves of good that flow your way. You'll have the extra energy to overflow to others, giving joyfully to those around you. The result is that you'll quite naturally find yourself making your world a better world.

When we give ourselves permission to truly embody this feeling of overflow, expansion, and real well-being, we find this is what was intended for us all along. It's our birthright to experience fulfillment, living life and relating to our children from this inner overflow. Parenting from this state is a completely different experience from parenting with an empty tank and struggling to do it well.

Make Self-Care Your Own

Self-care isn't one-size-fits-all. Rather, self-care is both individual and intimate. Self-care is about so much more than pampering. It's a response to a deep soul call within us to be quenched. Self-care is caring for our Innermost Self, our life on every level of consciousness: physical, mental, emotional and spiritual. Nourishing your spirit may look like learning to ask for what you need, going to therapy, working on your marriage, leaving a relationship, cleaning up your emotional baggage, learning to speak up for yourself, learning to speak respectfully to your children, facing addiction, losing weight, gaining weight, going back to school, changing careers, appreciating yourself or getting a massage.

Because self-care is meant to be a restorative bridge to assist us to move from one state of consciousness to a higher one, it's necessary to take the time to connect with our intuition and access what it is we need at any given moment. When we do so, we discover there's actually a wide palette we can benefit from. Just as an artist doesn't use only one or two colors, but chooses what feels appropriate at the moment from a large selection, it's important we too select just the right ways to supply our needs.

Inner-care is all about the quality of our life. I have learned that the *quality* of my life trumps the *form* of my life. Our culture teaches us to put what we are seeking first—the form ahead of quality, whether that be a relationship, marriage, money, a career, a salary or promotion—or where life with our children is concerned, the prestigious school and activities, good grades, getting them into bed at night or to brush their teeth. Not that these things aren't important. However, so many individuals create everything they have ever sought in terms of the outer form of life and yet, are often still inwardly empty. Good grades don't necessarily imply a love of learning. In contrast, when we embody the quality of life we are seeking, the form is guaranteed, because form always follows consciousness. The form may not always look the way we thought it would look, but when we embrace it, we find it amazingly fulfilling.

Not sure what kind of self-care you would enjoy? Then let me share some of the things I feel valuable—perhaps they will spark something in you. For me self-care includes all things inspirational: lighting candles in the evening, listening to music throughout the day, dancing to that music sometimes, singing with my son, taking bubble baths, picking flowers and taking the time to place them in rooms throughout my home, practicing uncensored writing when I feel upset, journaling, playing my piano, walking, nature, looking at the sunset, getting a massage, taking some quiet time by myself, helping out a friend, reading something inspirational, painting with my son, going to Agape (my spiritual community), taking a class, teaching a class, cleaning out a closet or a drawer, painting a room, watching a great movie or show, going to the symphony, participating in care circles with my friends, sharing gratitudes and acknowledgements, volunteering and finding a way to be of service and taking ME time daily.

I also derive benefit from self-care in the form of photo walks (walking with camera in hand!), walk-n-talks (inspirational and intentional talks with my husband or girlfriends), bike rides, eating popcorn for dinner, sleep, drinking lots of water, drinking water with lemon slices out of a beautiful wine glass, using the good china, yoga, spinning, hiking, crafting, knitting, drawing or coloring with my son, creating our own cards rather than buying them, wrapping our gifts in white paper so we can decorate them ourselves, and anything inspirational such as books, other writings, movies, or going to the mountaintop and embracing my feelings. I care for my physical body by drinking a protein shake every day, not eating emotionally or after 7 pm most of the time and taking the time to work out and stretch my body.

On a deeper level, inner-care is listening to and answering the call of my soul to create the life I have come here to live. Inner-care has looked like taking one hundred percent responsibility for my life, my emotional reactions and what I call "emotional self-care." I've learned to unpack the heavy emotional suitcase I'd been carrying from childhood and to pause when I'd find myself upset with my son. I've worked on and "cared for" my marriage. I've practiced risking in so many ways from participating in vulnerable conversations with friends, asking for what I need, saying no to what I don't want, drawing boundaries, letting go of the need for approval and giving myself my own approval. Mostly, I've transformed a consciousness based upon lack and "not-enoughness" to a life of gratitude and abundance. This is why I say that inner-care is not for the faint-of-heart! Yet, every mother I know is up for the challenge!

So, what are some simple but effective means of self-care that have been calling to you? Start off with what is simple, doable and right in front of you—that which takes no extra effort. You might wish to make a list of them—you may surprise yourself by how many there are. As you discover ways you enjoy engaging in self-care, I encourage you to calendar yourself in pen. Then take the simple step of committing to one of those ways *today*.

17

Invest in Yourself

Books about finances tell us the way to build wealth is to pay yourself first. Research shows that when you pay yourself first, you'll still have money for food as well as the rent or mortgage at the end of the month. But if you think you are going to save once all your bills are paid, by the end of the month you'll rarely find money left over for saving.

Can you recall times as a mother when you've told yourself something like, "I know I need to take care of myself, and I'll begin doing it right after…," and of course the "right after" is always about someone or something else. Inevitably you end up distracted, and then it's on to the next thing. Somehow you just never seem to get back to yourself. In contrast, when you take care of yourself *first*, you not only feel better, but you still have time and energy to care for those around you.

Especially as women and mothers, we are taught to find our value in giving to and doing for others. Caring for *ourselves* sends a message to our core self that we matter. People who value themselves cultivate both the courage and the confidence to live the life they are here to live. And as we've been seeing, ironically those who value themselves *are the first to care for others.*

Time to Treasure Yourself

Inner-care brings us an *awareness* that we are enough, lacking nothing. Additionally, it connects us with the infinite abundance of the universe, which is always available to us if we but connect with it. In a nutshell, self-care reminds us that we are supported *when we invest the time to support ourselves.*

Few have more on our "doing" plate than mothers. I have come to know that the more we take care of our "being," the more we have available to pour into our "doing." These days, I seek to fill my "being" tank before entering my "doing". After all, we wouldn't think of driving from Los Angeles to New York City with a fuel tank on empty. We would naturally fill up the tank first. Why would we imagine life itself is any different from how we so naturally take care of things like filling the fuel tank?

Self-care takes us beyond simple survival mode with our children. If we also take the time to clean the car inside and out, the *quality* of our ride is enhanced. It feels good to ride in a car that has been cared for both internally and externally. Well, life with our children is no different. When we enter this abundant state in which our being begins to inform our doing, the quality of our doing is enriched because it's infused with a joy that was all but absent before.

When my father taught me to drive, he told me not to let my tank go below half-full. Besides the fact that cars run more efficiently with a full tank, he didn't want me to end up stranded and running on empty. There's an anxiety that happens when our gas light comes on. So many of my clients first come to me running on empty and self-care for mothers is sometimes a tall order. I encourage my clients to seek to care for themselves eighty percent of the time, so that there is a reserve for those inevitable times when self-care is all but impossible.

As well, I encourage mothers to acknowledge and appreciate themselves when they do care for themselves rather than judging themselves when they don't. There'll be times when self-care isn't possible or appropriate. Self-judgment only depletes an already challenging habit to create. Self-appreciation fortifies what you have done and inspires more of the same.

Use Your Good China

My friend and great singer Carl Anderson used to say to me, "Life is short. Be sure to use your good china."

There's nothing like children to cause most mothers to put away their good china and take out the cheap plates—or even paper plates. Putting the good china and crystal away symbolizes how it's so easy for mothers to put their own spirit away when children are young.

It's true that using your good china and crystal will likely mean some breakages, but the message it sends to our children about valuing ourselves is priceless.

My son William makes a refreshing orange juice and sparkling water drink that he likes to serve in beautiful large wine glasses. He loves to offer a glass to guests when they arrive at our home, but he equally loves to serve it for us with dinner in the evenings. I enjoy drinking my morning tea from a real English teacup. We've broken many of both, but the pleasure we've received is incomparable.

Of course, using the good china and crystal is a metaphor for a way of being, bringing the best of ourselves out of the closet of our unconsciousness. There's nothing like caring for our spirit to usher the best parts of ourselves into life with our children.

My client Nancy is the mother of triplet boys, age six. As you can imagine, when she first came to me, self-care wasn't high on her list of priorities. She explained:

I loved the idea of nourishing my spirit. I knew my spirit was dying on the vine, buried beneath the day-to-day grind of caring for my boys. I had such a hard time with consistency. I'd get some momentum going, only to backslide and end up right where I started, overwhelmed and exhausted.

I knew their napping days were coming to an end, so I kept trying to nap while they napped. It just seemed to make sense and yet, deep down, I found myself wanting to *wake up*, so to speak, not go back to sleep.

On a practical level, I wanted a gym membership, but I didn't have the extra money or anyone to watch the boys. I ended up going to the thrift store and buying a stationary bike. It might sound dramatic to say, but that bike changed my life. I put the bike on my back patio with a pile of inspirational books I'd been wanting to read. I created a playlist of my favorite music and, for that hour a day, pedaled fast and furiously, infusing my mind with uplifting words. Although the bike was stationary, I began to feel that my life was going somewhere.

I noticed the inner feeling of exhilaration first. It just felt great to push my body. I lost some weight and stopped eating the crusts of the boys' sandwiches, calling it lunch. I actually took the time to make a salad for myself. As my body felt stronger and I felt better about myself, I found myself becoming more active with my boys. We'd go on bike rides together, and these rides became my lifeline to my spirit.

Buying that bike and immersing myself in some inspirational "me" time when my boys napped had an unexpected rippling effect on my life with them. The day I realized I'd been eating the leftovers on my boys' plates, calling them breakfast and lunch, was the day I started using my good china, so to speak. Nourishing my spirit had inspired me to nourish the rest of my life.

I treasured my time on my bike, then I'd treasure my time with my boys.

Inner-care will repeatedly stretch you beyond your comfort zone and catapult you forward in every area of your life. It will assist you in asking for what you truly want instead of being apologetic for wanting so much, while it will also empower you to say "no" to what you don't want, thereby enabling you to set clear boundaries.

Ask for What You Need

With families living further and further apart, it can be challenging for mothers to find the support necessary to take care of themselves while also caring for their children. Plus, society values those who do it all themselves. The individual who does the most receives the most accolades. Asking for support is seen as weak. Mothers are sometimes so busy focused upon the task in front of us, we can end up doing it all ourselves. And yet, ask we must when the situation calls for such.

In order to ask for what we want, we must first clarify what it is we need. This is sometimes difficult—especially for women and mothers, who have been taught to do for others without giving a thought for their own needs. You may want to become still for a moment, perhaps close your eyes, place your hands on your heart, and ask yourself what you need in this moment. This simple practice, done anytime, can be a powerful and transformative experience. When we take the time to lovingly ask, a loving answer will always come.

However, it's one thing to know you need something and quite another to actually ask to have that need met. Doing it all ourselves protects us from the vulnerability that sometimes comes with asking. However, asking for what we need in order to truly care for our life and nourish our spirit allows another to experience the good feeling of giving. This is mutuality.

Whenever we practice such mutuality, it creates deeper intimacy in our life—not only as we take the risk of asking, but also as we allow the other into our heart and life on a deeper level than may have felt comfortable in the past. The willingness and courage to ask for what we need grows us into the humble, connected, interdependent beings we are here to be.

My client Sophia shared her experience of being a new mom to her daughter Isabella:

When Isabella is tired and cranky and ready for bed, I sometimes find myself skipping my own self-care routine at night. I rush through brushing my teeth, if I brush them at all. I tell myself that not washing my face won't kill me.

I realized how difficult it was for me to ask my husband Luca to hold his own daughter. I felt like I was asking too much. After all, he'd worked all day just like I had. However, I began to ask him to hold Isabella a little while longer so I could slow down and actually floss! Throw in some minty mouthwash and some lip balm, and I felt so much better the rest of the night.

Luca hadn't seen Isabella all day, so he was happy to spend some time connecting with her. Even though he's tired from work, he is energized around Isabella. To have him care for her turned out not to be the burden I perceived it to be. To him, time with Isabella in the evening is what makes his day.

It's seems so super tiny, but I think it's those zillions of little cut corners that lead to personal neglect.

If we are to live a purposeful life that reaches for our highest vision, asking for what we need is a skill we must cultivate. The surface discomfort we may initially experience pales in comparison with the deeper, rich feeling of being true to our highest self. As Shakespeare's Polonius said so poignantly, "To thine own self be true."

With this in mind, perhaps consider what one thing you could ask for today to assist you in growing on your spiritual path. Does asking cause you to feel vulnerable? Are you willing to ask anyway?

Engage in Gracious Receiving

Giving and receiving are ultimately the same energy. But if this is the case, why is it sometimes so much easier for some of us to give than to receive?

Receiving can put us in the position of revealing ourselves more transparently than we typically feel comfortable doing. Receiving may also feel selfish—or, as we noted earlier, weak, because our culture acknowledges those who "do it all by themselves."

Authentic giving results from an overflow. Many of us give, but because the giving is based in a sense of lack and obligation, the feeling—the *tone*—behind the giving is that of resentment, inner constriction, and contraction. Giving that comes from an expanded, spacious, overflowing energy is true, selfless giving. We are enlivened when we give from a heart of love for others.

When we care for ourselves enough to give graciously from our overflow, we model to our children to do the same. Children are born generous givers and they learn to withhold that giving from the world. Generous giving from an overflow is restorative to the soul and is life affirming and relationship building.

The fact is that we are interdependent beings who thrive on supporting each other. This is the state of mutuality, experiencing the two-way benefit of true giving and receiving, the hallmark of healthy relationships and families. A natural elation arises when we give and receive support because in that act we are being true to our nature.

Healthy Boundaries

Setting healthy boundaries sometimes involves saying "no" to what we *don't* want. Most of us, especially women and mothers, tend to feel guilty when saying "no" to something we know isn't even lined up for us. We often say "yes" when we really mean "no," especially to our children, then live a life that's out of alignment with our core values.

Dr. Shefali Tsabary, author of *The Conscious Parent*, on one of her recent tele classes, shared a powerful example from her own life. Her daughter really wanted a dog, and yet Dr. Shefali knew that, as a mother, she herself wasn't prepared to have a dog in their family. Rather than saying yes to her daughter when she really meant no, then harboring resentment about the dog, she found the courage to let her daughter know that it wasn't something she could do at this time. Uncomfortable as it might have been, Dr. Shefali found the inner courage to have her actions align with her core values.

Giving ourselves permission to ask for what we need as well as to say "no" when we mean no is essential to create a healthy family life. It's so important to model to our children that we can ask for what we need in this world and take up the space that we are here to inhabit. Equally important it is for them to experience us aligned with our core values when our answer is no.

If you are concerned about the reaction someone may have when you set a boundary, to do so can feel intimidating.

When we take a moment to become still, most of us know deep down when a healthy boundary needs to be established. Often, however, we override our intuition either because we fear another's reaction or because of rigid rules internalized from our past. For instance, women are sometimes afraid to be seen as pushy, bossy, or selfish, and so they don't give themselves permission to set healthy boundaries. They don't want to be seen to "take up too much space." As seen in the example above, mothers can feel guilty to say no to their children and abandon their own inner wisdom just to avoid this uncomfortable feeling or the reaction of their children. Yet, nowhere is having the courage to set and carry out healthy boundaries more important than in our life with our children, as children need this healthy containment to thrive.

Mother's Intuition

There's nothing more powerful than inner-care to connect you to your intuition. Inner-care connects you to a higher energy where answers, solutions, guidance, and wisdom become clear and easily accessible. The more familiar you become with this crystalline energy, the more you'll lean into it and live from it on a day-to-day basis.

My client Emily shared how something as simple as arranging flowers introduced her daughter, Grace to the higher power of her intuition:

I've been cutting fresh flowers on Sundays and placing them in a beautiful vase on our dining room table. At first I honestly didn't think it would make a difference to my week, but I did it anyway. When I walk into my house in the evenings, the flowers just light up my heart. I never expected that a simple vase of flowers would bring me so much joy.

Last month I wasn't feeling well, so Grace went out and brought in the flowers for us. Coming from a fourteen-year-old girl who's wrapped up in her friends and social life, this simple act surprised me. She took such care arranging the flowers. When she was done, she commented that she'd like to arrange them from now on. She shared a situation concerning one of her best friends that was upsetting to her, and how, while arranging the flowers, she worked out what she was going to say to her friend.

After that, she'd arrange the flowers and simultaneously work out different school and friend situations. Time after time, she's able to connect with her own inner knowing of how to handle situations. Our conversations feel just like these beautiful flowers look. It's delightful to connect to my teenage daughter in this heartfelt way. Those lovely flowers brought each of us so much more than we would have expected.

When we take the risk, set a boundary and follow our intuition, we experience the well-being that comes as a result of being true to ourselves. This feeling of well-being puts us in the wheelhouse of abundance, with access to all of the resources we need to fulfill our destiny. People, situations, unexpected gifts, and unexpected good rush our way providing for us exactly what we need—and more.

18

Mothers Who Meditate

Have you heard the saying that the longest journey in life is the journey from the head to the heart?

Although I've had a consistent meditation practice since I was about sixteen years old, it was when I had a child that meditation became non-negotiable in my life. I realized early on in my sleep-deprived state that nothing of this world (not even sleep!) could restore me to the level I sought to parent from in the way meditation did. Even a short meditation can rejuvenate the spirit in a way nothing else does.

At the same time, I also learned that a meditation practice often needs to look different for a mother than for many. Over and over, I see with my mom clients that when they give themselves permission to create a meditation practice that works for them and their lifestyle, rather than try to fit their meditation practice into a prescribed box that they think it is supposed to look like, they are able to implement it with more consistency. Because they are consistent, the results always seem to surpass what they thought would be possible.

A traditional meditation practice seeks to quiet the mind, which often proves challenging for the overactive minds of the West. Add to this the overactive mind of the western mother, who is plagued with the endless list of things that need to be done for her child. The reality is, it's nearly impossible for a mother to receive the benefits she was looking for when she began a meditation practice in the first place.

Because we are a results-driven society, whereas meditation is a process-oriented experience, meditation can be challenging particularly for mothers. The fact is, it isn't always easy for westerners to simply sit still and "be" present with themselves. Even when mothers do take a few moments to sit in stillness, they sometimes feel overwhelmed with their "to do" lists that aren't getting done or they feel pressure to find bliss and reach nirvana in those few quiet moments. Consequently they end up frustrated and give up on their meditation practice. It all comes down to not knowing that they need to make it their own—to do it in a way that works for them.

Most mothers are trying to find the "right" way to meditate. We think it needs to look like sitting still for 20 minutes with a quiet mind. I always start by diminishing the amount of time a mother needs to meditate. When mothers give themselves permission to meditate for five minutes rather than thirty-five minutes, those five minutes provide such a restorative energy that they naturally want more of that experience.

When I used to teach piano to children, the question I got asked by parents more than any other question was how to get their children to practice. I told them that if they wanted their child to practice for thirty minutes, stop them after fifteen. If their child got fidgety after ten minutes, stop them after five minutes. Allow them a rich experience and then leave them wanting more. Provide yourself a rich experience with meditation and leave yourself wanting more. Better to sit for five blissful minutes in the bathroom with the door closed and want more, than try to sit for forty minutes in your chair in the bedroom and never make it through to the end.

Do I encourage parents to meditate before their children wake up in the morning? Of course. But what if you aren't a morning person or are still tired when you awaken after a sleepless night with one or more of your children? Also, it's so easy to persuade ourselves we need to wait until the moment is perfect and the space is clear, so that our meditation can be a beautiful experience.

This is all quite understandable. Except that when we finally have the courage to jettison all the ways we *think* meditation is supposed to look and find our own approach as mothers, we free ourselves to actually experience the benefits meditation can bring.

Once we let go of all of the rules of meditation, we tend to find ourselves spontaneously drawn to create a simple, uncluttered space, perhaps with a few meaningful items that visually evoke the inner feeling, tone, and intention that meditation brings. Perhaps we gift ourselves with five minutes of stillness rather than waiting for the thirty minutes that rarely come. Then as we experience the benefits of a calmer nervous system, emotional equanimity, and a heart that's both peaceful and grateful, we may be drawn to wake up ahead of our children, even if it's only by five minutes. In other words, if meditation is to become a part of your life, let it happen organically. In this way the benefits you experience from meditation create the desire to give the practice a more prominent role in your life.

It's About Opening Your Heart

Our relationship with our "self" is the most intimate relationship we will ever have. Meditation is meant to set up the conditions to quiet the mind so that we can experience *being* with ourselves. Meditation is one of the most powerful technologies we have to create awareness of this union with ourselves. It can go a long way to restoring us to our true nature.

A full heart invites an illumined mind. For this reason, in my work with clients over the years, especially mothers with our endless "to do" lists and tasks, I have learned that rather than trying to quiet the mind, a more effective approach is to focus on opening the heart. Our mind seeks to fix things, whereas our heart seeks to embrace. Residing in our heart allows the stress, pressure, and anxiety that a mother places on herself to easily and gracefully fall away.

For many of my clients, as well as for myself, there's nothing better than music to quiet the mind and open the heart. Putting on a beautiful piece of music helps me relax into my heart. The music allows me to, as it were, "exhale." Perhaps especially in the case of a mother, appropriate music has the power to invite her to shed a boatload of tears she's been storing away.

Guided meditations can also be helpful for mothers as well as for our children. Because it can be challenging to settle ourselves down, listening to a guided meditation does the "work" for us, allowing us to relax and receive. We connect with our naturally abundant state easiest when we're most relaxed. Five minutes with a piece of music or a guided meditation creates a rich atmosphere for the soul to be restored. When we feed our heart in this way, we experience the abundance that's our natural state. Live from your abundance, and your entire relationship with your children is enhanced.

How to Meditate Around Young Children

I can't tell you how many people who have tried meditation tell me, "I have such a problem focusing." My response is that there's nothing like meditating with a child crawling over your legs or asking you "how much longer?" to cultivate the muscle of focus.

Remember how we talked in an earlier chapter about how our children come into our life to help us grow? There's no better moment to discover this than, as you settle down to meditate, using the noise and distractions all around you to your advantage. At this moment, *they* are your teacher.

A key aspect of becoming an effective meditator is learning to be (if I may be permitted to coin a word) "undistractable." The beautiful thing is that if we are persistent with our practice, in spite of and in the midst of the activity of our children, over time these very same children will morph into beings who are supportive of our practice.

I never asked my son to be quiet or still while I meditated when he was young. Yet after a while he learned to come snuggle up beside me for a few moments. Then he was off to his next adventure, and perhaps a little while later back on my lap. He would come and go as he pleased, sometimes gently and sometimes intrusively, but I always welcomed him with open arms and a loving heart. At least I was meditating, even if the atmosphere wasn't pristine. The wonderful payoff of not fighting what's happening around you is that it tends to be catching. At twelve, meditation is just a part of my son's life as it's been a part of mine.

Bedtime and down time are other times to choose meditation. As we said, bedtime is typically a moment when we mothers are running on fumes. Use the time when you are lying down next to your children to connect with your *own* heart and Spirit. By the end of the day, our Spirit is usually the last thing we think about connecting with, but the very thing that will restore us. Take some deep breaths and allow yourself to meditate while your child is falling asleep. You may not always be sitting up straight with your feet flat upon the floor, but you will be connecting with your essence and sourcing yourself in a way that nothing else possibly can.

I encourage mothers to meditate throughout the day, even if it doesn't look like a formal meditation practice. Use opportunities like when your child is napping or at school, or when you are doing the dishes. Many mothers I work with set the alarm on their watch and meditate at the top of the hour a few times during the day. I love meditating when my son takes a shower at night. The sound of the water is soothing and those few moments become restorative for the rest of my evening.

I also encourage mothers to take 5 minutes with their child and sit quietly together. Turn on some quiet music or a guided meditation. Even if it isn't formal, your child will stay connected to their natural rhythm, inner wisdom and Spirit by implementing this practice into their life. One of my clients calls this time with her child "cuddle-tation."

Many of my clients are working mothers. I encourage them to take even five minutes in their car before coming home from work to be still and connect with their spirit. Just as a man comes home and sometimes changes his clothes to transition into the evening of being with the family, it is important for mothers to give ourselves permission to transition. Even five minutes of meditation before reentering the home can change the tone of your entire evening. So toss out the "rules" of meditation and discover how a quiet moment isn't better than a noisy one and that any meditation is better than no meditation.

Meditation As a Portal

The thing that makes for quality parenting is the place inside ourselves, we are parenting *from*. Inner-care and meditation connect us to an infinite presence, which allows us to live and parent from abundance and calm rather than lack, fear and frenzy.

When we parent from abundance, we are open to the infinite possibilities in a situation, even the most challenging ones. When we parent from lack, which is an issue of fear, we see only limited choices—that is, if we see any choices at all. We are constricted rather than expanded, and we inevitably project our fears onto our children. Using meditation for self-care transforms the quality of our consciousness. The energy we experience then draws our children to us, rather than pushing them away from us as we tend to do when we feel depleted. It's all a matter of changing the energy within ourselves.

For many of my clients, myself included, meditation becomes a portal to a fulfilled life. We find it to be a gateway to awareness. The more aware we are, the more we realize how the universe works in countless, often unnoticed, ways to increase our well-being.

At its best, meditation expands from a practice in which we cloister ourselves away for so many minutes at a time into a way of life. The awareness we gain and the presence we touch during meditation infuses itself into every aspect of our everyday life, especially life with our children. We are seeking to bring our expanded awareness and our insightful and enlightened moments into our relationship with our children. We find that there are spaces in between the doing that become apparent and available. We are seeking to bring that energy into the atmosphere of our home and time with our children.

Our children can intuitively feel our own inner shifts in energy. They feel the energy underneath our words and tone, just as we felt the energy underneath our parents' words in the environment of our own homes growing up. We are seeking to plug ourselves into the outlet of inspiration and shine that light into our homes and onto our relationships with our children.

As our awareness expands, so does our capacity for self-care.

19

Practices that Will Enrich Your Life

I'd like to share with you some of the key practices my clients and I have found become a part of our lives as we engage in self-care and increasingly see its value. These practices revolve around gratitude, appreciation, forgiveness, selfless service and experiencing joie de vivre.

Gratitude

I consider gratitude to be the grandfather of all spiritual practice, and an unparalleled practice where our life with children is concerned. As with self-care, gratitude opens the portal to abundance and the true giving-ness of life. A gratitude practice invites us to *reside in our essence* because it puts us in contact with what is truly important in life. Both of these are so essential in raising children that remain intrinsically connected to the generosity of the universe and to their own essence and generosity of spirit.

When we create a practice of seeking out that which is within us and around us to be grateful for, we cultivate a consciousness of abundance. We cultivate a consciousness that looks for what is working, rather than what isn't, what is there is rather than what seems to be lacking. We create habits of seeing and expressing gratitude for the abundance all around us and for our very life itself. It's because authentic gratitude is a "mode of being" in everyday life, rather than simply something we express from time to time either in words or actions, that its power to transform our life is unparalleled.

We can practice gratitude anytime, anywhere. It doesn't cost anything. At any moment, we can stop and choose to count our blessings. And, in fact, when we take the time to look for blessings, we indeed find them. I can't imagine a day going by without expressing my gratitude out loud to and with my son. Even in the middle of challenges, we learn that we are multidimensional beings, capable of experiencing human emotions and profound gratitude all at the same time.

Gratitude is such a simple, but powerful practice to engage in with our children. In our home we have a gratitude wall. It is simply a large sheet of art paper that we decorate and have markers on a table nearby. It starts off as a blank canvas and whenever one of us walks by, we write down something that we are grateful for or that we appreciate about another in the family. It's so neat to walk by and see another family member's gratitude. It's also such a good feeling to write gratitudes on the page and watch it fill up with things that are meaningful to each one of us.

Many families have gratitude practices at the dinner table or before bed at night. There is nothing like going around a table listening and expressing gratitudes from the day. Even the youngest of children instantly understands and can participate in this practice. It gives everyone involved such a good feeling.

"If the only prayer you ever say in your entire life is thank you, it will be enough." said Meister Eckhart. I find this to be so true that I consider gratitude the highest form of prayer. I notice that whenever our son begins a prayer, he always begins with something he is grateful for. In fact, his prayers usually consist only of gratitude.

Gratitude is an indirect way to teach manners. When gratitude is a way of life, saying please and thank you comes naturally out of a child's mouth. The words are then infused with the actual feeling of gratitude underneath the words, rather than the rote words parroted by many children.

Engaging in daily practices of gratitude also cultivates magnanimity. When we are truly grateful, we naturally go out of our way for others or do that little extra unnecessary, but greatly appreciated something. For instance, last week was our son's birthday. He wrote thank you cards for his gifts and unexpectedly, when opening the mail yesterday, there was a thank you card he had written to my husband and me, filled with gratitude that he took the time to express to us. William has stayed connected to his generous spirit, and also his grateful heart.

When we take the time to be thankful, our heart opens and expands to include gratitude for every aspect of life. For this reason, gratitude is the gateway to abundance.

Gratitude in Challenging Situations

Gratitude is such a powerful practice to cultivate in the midst of challenging situations. When we ask the question, "What good is seeking to be revealed in this situation?" we expand our consciousness to see not only the challenge in front of us, but also other unseen aspects of the situation.

For instance, a client of mine, Beverly, was having a challenge with her teenage son, Ryan. Often when they would spend time together, things would start off well, but at some point, one or both of them would end up frustrated about something, usually involving the other person. Beverly asked herself what good was seeking to emerge from this situation. She began looking for the good in the midst of her discomfort.

Beverly first became grateful that Ryan, a young man of 16, even wanted to spend time together. She realized that as her son got older, he didn't have to choose to spend time with her and that if she wanted their relationship to continue there were ways that she was being asked to evolve as a person that he would choose to be around. She saw the

long standing adversarial pattern between them and recognized a soft-
ness and gentleness that was seeking to emerge within her for *herself.*
So much of her inner energy was harsh and critical and she knew it was
time to befriend herself in the way that Ryan was seeking an alley.

Because Beverly asked this question, so much good came to her relationship with Ryan. She was able to share with Ryan what she was
learning about herself. In fact, Beverly has commented quite often the
depth of gratitude she has for Ryan for being such a great teacher for
her. She found gratitude in the midst of a challenging situation.

Beverly also shared with me that because of this practice of asking
what good is seeking to emerge in a challenging situation, she is able
to assist her other children in their lives as well. When her daughter
Emma was having a challenge with a friend at school, Beverly was able
to listen to Emma with an open and patient heart. There was no rush to
fix or change anything about the situation. Beverly was grateful to simply listen to Emma.

Beverly was then able to assist Amelia to look for the good that was
seeking to emerge from the situation. Emma found a voice for herself
and spoke up to her friend about her feelings. Her friend was able to
share with her some deeper feelings and the girls are closer than ever.
They both learned patience, tolerance, effective self-expression and authentic sharing. They're both grateful for the challenging situation that
ultimately brought them closer because they chose to look for the good
that was there in its midst all along.

Asking what good is seeking to emerge in the midst of a challenging
situation teaches our children that they don't need to avoid uncomfortable situations and circumstances in life. It teaches them to be empowered by facing the situation and looking for the unseen good that is within it in potential.

It isn't such a leap to imagine different cultures and even countries
learning to get along because of a gratitude practice. Gratitude expands

our world and creates an internal sense of overflowing fullness that completely changes how we see a challenging situation.

Gratitude is a Process

Becoming a grateful person is for many of us a process. So, how can we nurture a grateful state of mind?

I once heard it said that the Dalai Lama meditates each morning as if that day might be his last day on Earth. Naturally, this prepares him to live the day to the fullest. Don't we all want to live life to the fullest, the way we would if we knew that today would be our last day on Earth?

When something occurs that we consider tragic—such as a six-week-old infant dies, or a mother of a child of four is killed in an automobile crash—the way we process, or fail to process, such a situation determines whether we will be able to experience a measure of gratitude in it.

Unless we are in great pain of some sort, whether physical or emotional, do any of us care to even really think about dying? After working with so many individuals, I believe we seek to avoid thoughts of death *to the degree we are not fully living*. I find that the more fully someone is engaged in their life, the less resistance they have to contemplating death. For this reason, something paradoxical happens when we consider our own dying. Coming face to face with the fact that we will ultimately pass from life puts us in touch with the degree to which we are actually living our life in each moment.

Whenever I'm courageous enough to embark on a conversation around death, I experience some of the most intimate moments with clients. The conversation always seems to circle back to their innermost desire to experience—to really *inhabit*—the preciousness of life, which is something we so often take for granted in our everyday living.

We also become aware of how fleeting our life really is in the larger scheme of eternity. We see that our time with our children is limited and therefore, becomes that much more precious when we experience it in this way. When I recognize that my son won't always be living at home with us, I become more deeply grateful for each moment that he is here with us.

The thought of my own passing, connecting me to my innermost desire to savor my life fully, now becomes ironically liberating. I walk the Earth with full awareness of my eventually passing, and by carrying this awareness within me—not wearing it as a heavy burden—I seek to live each day to the fullest. Consequently I increasingly find myself cherishing the life that has been entrusted to me.

What Gratitude Really Involves

Being able to be grateful in even the painful episodes in life really gets to the heart of what gratitude is. Gratitude isn't solely about counting just our blessings, as we are so often reminded to do, but about living from our essence—the very heart of ourselves, which is simply thrilled to *be,* since our spiritual center knows that life is about more than having enjoyable experiences. Think of a young child. They are just thrilled to *be.* Gratitude reconnects us to our childlike nature and the true joy of being alive. Gratitude is about having an undefended heart that's open to and thankful for the entirety of the adventure of being human.

Paradoxically, nothing draws more good into our lives than an undefended heart. When our heart is open and receptive, the natural abundance of the universe is able to flow to us. So it is that many of the kinds of blessings we all like to "count" do in fact have a way of flooding into our life.

Within the family, connection and intimacy is created when we express gratitude. For instance, sitting around the table or lying in bed at night expressing gratitude enables us to hear what's truly important to our children. When I allow my son to just talk and express what he's grateful for, I get to peek inside him. I'm often surprised by the things he's grateful for, which are sometimes quite different from the things I imagine he would be grateful for. I get to see the world from his point of view, so that I know him better and understand what's meaningful to him. At the same time, he feels more seen by me. When we share with each other in an honest and authentic way like this, we feel connected.

I once read an article about the Obamas and their practice called "roses and thorns," a practice we adopted in our family. Seated around the table, we take turns to express the good things (the roses), followed by the day's thorns. It's an indirect way of assisting a child to become expressive about their life, including about what is or isn't working for them. It's become a powerful form of connection in our family.

On many occasions William not only shares thorns, but thorns that "turned into roses." In reality, he finds the rose that's among the thorns all along. What's happening is that because I'm simply listening without having an agenda that involves fixing or solving a problem, he finds his own way to work things out in his world. More times than not, this leads to discovering his own blessings in a situation. It's so empowering for our children to navigate through their challenges and discover gems of gratitude waiting for them.

Appreciation

It's been said that what we appreciate, appreciates. If there's one practice that can propel us out of a sense of lack and "not enoughness," to coin an expression, it's the practice of appreciation. It shifts us from disconnection and fear toward the energy of abundance, connection, joy, and even bliss.

You might think that gratitude and appreciation are much the same, but there's actually quite a difference. Appreciation isn't just a matter of being grateful for someone or something, but is *the act of holding someone or something in high regard*. It's the opposite of finding fault, criticizing, and constantly correcting.

Mary Beth, a client, had been including this practice of appreciation in her self-care. Mary Beth was working with the harsh ways she criticized her daughter, Paula. She had come to realize that the way she related to her daughter reflected the ways she felt herself to be "not enough", failing and lacking as a mother. There'd been constant tension between them. Not a day passed without Mary Beth making some kind of judgmental comment about Paula.

She shared with me an experience she had with Paula in ice skating class. It was a turning point in how she regarded her daughter, as she herself explained:

As Paula got on the ice, I settled in on the bench and took out my phone to answer emails. Every few minutes, I looked up to see how she was doing. She smiled and I went back to my phone. But at some point I began to sense I should put away my phone and watch her. It was like an inner urging to be present with her—my Mother's Intuition that I've disregarded so many times in the past that I am now learning to honor. So I moved over to the plexiglass that surrounded the rink and observed as she took her lesson.

At first it was sweet, as she was so excited to have me watch. Then I became aware of the thoughts that were going through my head as I watched her skate. "Why isn't she bending her knees? She needs to bend her knees more. Why is she so stiff? She needs to loosen up. She's so afraid to fall."

As I observed these thoughts. I could see where they were headed. They were all marching toward a definite conclusion about my horrible parenting. "What did you do wrong that she is so afraid to fail? She will never dare to do anything if she plays it safe her whole life."

The more I became aware of the nature of these thoughts, the more I realized they were an outdated knee-jerk reaction that didn't really feel like "me" anymore—that is, the "me" I've come to know through my practice of appreciation. I could feel the old constricted energy wanting to give way to the new expansive me. I wanted to breathe in the breath of fresh air I'd been experiencing in my life lately. I did, in fact, take a deep breath.

I began appreciating myself for simply putting my phone down and walking over to the plexiglass to be present with Paula. I appreciated myself for the layers of self-judgment I'd shed and for my desire to have a connected relationship with Paula. These three simple but real appreciations literally shifted the rest of my experience at practice.

As I looked around at all the other kids, I saw that they each had their own abilities along with their own quirks. Each was doing their own thing. Questions popped into my head. What was the point of this class? What was I expecting from it? Did I want to take Paula all the way to the Olympics, or did I want her to get out on the ice and have fun, maybe learning a thing or two in the process? I realized that this wasn't my class, this wasn't my experience. It was hers. Maybe I could just let her have her own experience without trying to manage it to assuage my own old sense of not being good enough.

This is where the miraculous thing happened. As I let go of all of that, I began to see her differently. Not only did I see her differently, I could feel my appreciation of her well up within me. I appreciated how hard she was concentrating, the focus she was giving to what she was doing. I appreciated her sweetness and the encouragement she offered the other kids. I appreciated her enthusiasm and courage as she jumped into the circle and did a little dance move at the end of the class. As soon as my vision wasn't clouded by what I thought she—or more accurately, I—should be, I could appreciate how magnificent she truly was. I could see *her, just* her.

She came off the ice and ran toward me saying, "Mommy, I love ice skating! I want to take it twice a week. Let me show you these two moves I learned." And she demonstrated her moves. It was perfection—an uncluttered moment, clear and unfiltered.

I saw how it could have gone had I not been as aware—had I not been practicing appreciating *myself* in a pure and uncluttered way. When she came off the ice, I would likely have made a well-meaning "suggestion" about how she should bend her knees more next time. She would have felt the judgement hidden within it. She wouldn't have known that it was truly my own self-judgment. How could she? And even if it was only in a small way, I would have taken the wind out of her sails. Instead, we shared a moment of exuberance I will always remember.

Imagine knowing you are being held in high regard by someone. Then imagine how good it feels to hold yourself in high regard. When we appreciate ourselves, we begin to notice ourselves appreciating those around us, especially our children.

Give Yourself a Break

Appreciation is a crucial aspect of inner-care. You can see this in the case of Anne, another of my clients. "Before I did something for myself," said told me, "I thought I needed to do something for everyone else first, and then I'd do something for myself."

When Anne was a child, her mother had cancer; and since she was the oldest, it fell to her to care for both her mother and her little brother. Because she was so focused on caring for the members of her family, she never learned to care for herself.

Anne's father had extremely high expectations of her. As she increasingly internalized his voice, she came to have high expectations of herself. For instance, when she first started seeing me, she couldn't even give herself permission not to play with her two-year-old daughter now and then. Since her daughter wanted her attention all the time, she didn't feel she deserved a moment to herself.

Today, simply giving herself permission not to expect herself to be perfect—permission *not* to play with her daughter all the time—and owning her *choice* not to do so, is actually giving Anne a sense of spaciousness—and, as a result, a new joy and playfulness when she *is* with her daughter.

As Anne has discovered, inner-care looks like "giving myself a break." In fact, to use her words, "Self-care means not giving myself a hard time about everything." She adds, "Since I've learned that it's okay not to expect myself to be one-thousand percent at work and at home, ironically I'm experiencing the energy and enthusiasm to do more and procrastinate less. I would never have imagined this."

For Anne, the practice of appreciation involved becoming aware of all she was already doing as a single mother. As long as her focus was on everything she *wasn't* doing, she felt depleted of not only energy but enthusiasm for what she was doing. But when she began to appreciate all she was accomplishing, she felt increasingly energized.

To be able to say to herself, "Of course you are tired—you just worked a nine-hour day and are going home to care for your daughter," has helped Anne to realize that she quite naturally appreciates her daughter when she appreciates herself.

Anne is learning what appreciating herself sounds like: "Yes, look, you've worked a full day. It's okay to be tired. It's okay that dinner isn't a two-hour gourmet production. I appreciate myself for all that I *am* doing." In the past, she thought that what she needed to do to be a "good" mother was prepare such dinners, lest her daughter be disappointed, when really her daughter could care less about a gourmet dinner. As Anne put it, "She just wants my boob, anyway!"

Appreciation is a simple practice that yields profound results in all our relationships, especially with our children. Rather than something we say or do, it's a way of seeing ourselves and therefore others. There's nothing our children want more than to be seen by us. When we practice seeing and appreciating ourselves, we naturally see and appreciate them.

Also, appreciate yourself for your willingness to reconnect with something that may have been removed from your everyday life and may even seem impossible to revive. Appreciate yourself for your willingness to reconnect anyway. Appreciate yourself for breathing new life into your existence. Appreciate yourself for trusting that you can raise a family and raise yourself at the same time.

The practice of expressing appreciation is so powerful that I encourage the mothers I work with to express at least five things that they appreciate about themselves and five things they appreciate about their children each day. These can be simple everyday things like appreciating yourself for taking the time to really look into your child's eyes, appreciating yourself for trusting your intuition when making a decision, or appreciating yourself for listening to a friend who needed an ear. As is the case with gratitude, when you begin an appreciation practice, you'll find yourself looking for things to appreciate about yourself, as well as about your children.

Write those five things about yourself and your children in your journal and say it out loud to yourself. Share your appreciations of your children directly to your child each day. For older children who have phones and computers, you can text and e-mail. You can write the appreciations in a note and include in your child's lunch, but in some way, express the appreciation directly to your child each day. We model to them through our own appreciation of them.

Valuing ourselves and our children moves us out of the lack and limitation mentality and assists us to grow deep roots of abundance. Taking the time to share with your child a few things you appreciate about them each day communicates that you see and value them. You hold them in high regard, which is an important step toward creating an authentic connection in your relationship. When our children feel seen and valued, they will naturally see and value themselves and those around them as well.

Forgiveness

There are few areas of my life in which I find the need for forgiveness more than on my motherhood journey. It's so easy to see my stumbles rather than my triumphs, then to judge my missteps. Yet when I view my least attractive mothering moments not through the eyes of my own self-judgment but from the mountaintop with eyes of soft compassion, the need for forgiveness falls away.

We somehow think that our judgment of something is what makes it right or wrong. For example, we imagine that by judging a burglar, we are saying that his action is "wrong." The fact is, his action is his action, regardless of our reaction to it. I've learned that my judgment of an individual or a situation can neither add value to it nor detract from it. If there's to be value in something, I must be in a mindset that, as Albert Einstein said, doesn't meet the problem at the level of the problem.

When I judge another, in a sense I'm only exposing my own inner turbulent world. A peaceful person isn't the one who experiences road rage, right? My judgment is an indicator of my own internal disturbance. Therefore, before I can be of assistance to another, I must settle my own inner road rage, so to speak. As we saw earlier, the aspects of ourselves that are most disenfranchised are the very things that are calling out for us to give them love.

Again, this is best accomplished from the mountaintop, since it's there that we can provide ourselves with a bird's-eye view of our reaction to a situation. From the mountaintop, I remember that I'm not in any way bound—that there's no ceiling above me. I'm connected to an infinite presence that's larger than myself—larger than any situation I could possibly find myself in. When I recognize this about myself, I become an infinite container of compassion—not, at least initially, for another, but for myself. This infinite container of compassion encompasses my judgments, so that I look upon them with eyes of kindness.

When I look down from the mountain, I can see that I'm operating the best that I can in the situation. This enables me to provide my judgments with the caring and nurturing they crave from me. I can say empathically, "I see that you are judging because you think you need to protect me. I see that beneath your armor, you are hurting." When I speak in a compassionate way to myself, I find my armored state begins to soften.

This is the essence of forgiveness—the showing of my own love to myself. And because all judgment is ultimately self-judgment, I can say that all forgiveness is self-forgiveness. Without judgment, the need for forgiveness dissolves.

"It was a hectic morning, as so many of them are," my client Audry shared with me, going on to explain:

I was driving the carpool, and all the carpool kids were waiting outside, looking on, as I was yelling to my daughter to get her stuff and get to the car. I was going to visit a friend in the hospital directly after I dropped them off at school, so I was rushed and couldn't find my phone. My husband tried to help, but I got more and more short with him as well as my daughter. I became frantic, and the facade of the mom who has it all together fell quite dramatically and publicly. I felt like a crazy woman. In the end, I had to leave without my phone.

All the kids were strapped in, and as I pulled out of the driveway, I saw the look in the other mom's eye. She looked kind of scared that I had her kids in the car. I slowed down, took a deep breath, and drove slowly down the street, telling myself that none of this was a big deal. None of it. So I didn't have my phone—it wasn't the end of the world. I'd get directions to the hospital from someone at school. I slowly and methodically went through the various steps of my plan B, taking deep breaths as I did so.

I dropped the kids off, sighed a giant sigh, and as I was walking to my car, thought of a place in my bag I hadn't checked. Sure enough, my phone was there. I sat in my car and called the other mom to let her know we had gotten there safely and to apologize for my craziness.

She was understanding, and I should have felt relieved. Except that I didn't. I was convinced she secretly thought I was a crazy person, and I couldn't stop berating myself. I drove to the hospital, but before I went in, I sat in the parking lot, called into your tele class, and when the time came for sharing, chimed right in with what was going on with me. I was trying to forgive myself, but I couldn't seem to do it.

As you worked with me, I realized that the reason no amount of re-assurance from the other mom seemed to make me feel better was that *I* was the one who thought I was crazy. The judgment was coming from me, and I was projecting it onto her. So no amount of reassurance from her could ever make a difference. I had to look at my own feelings about myself, the impossible standards I set for myself, and how I judge myself so harshly when I make mistakes. I needed to learn to simply be present with all of this without trying to fix everything I think's wrong with myself. I needed to give it space and be present with the beliefs that animate it. As I allowed myself to be present with all of my high standards, self-judgments, and self-criticisms, feelings of compassion and self-forgiveness began to flow.

It's the judgments that need our forgiveness. Everyone makes mistakes, but it's the way I judge my mistakes that ultimately needs forgiveness.

The waves of self-compassion I now felt were so liberating. Self-forgiveness is an expansive and freeing process that reconnects us to our pure and innocent essence.

Joie de Vivre

A client, Shadi, said to me, "The quality that I think self-care brings to parenting is *joy*. As I mull the concept over, it occurs to me that taking care of myself opens up more joy to be shared with my family. It also occurs to me that while the 'doing' is important for mothering, the 'being' is even more important. I find when I'm 'being' loving and compassionate, I slow down and don't get caught up in the 'rush' of getting things 'done.' That may be the key for me when it comes to understanding how to *be* caring of myself."

I love the way Shadi said she was coming to understand how to *be* caring. It's so easy for self-care to become another item on a lengthy to-do list, which defeats the whole purpose. Self-care is a way of life, not a "doing." I have seen with my clients how two people can perform the same task, yet with an entirely different effect because one is engaging in a "doing" whereas the other is simply being.

To illustrate, cleaning out a closet for one person may be an important act of self-care. They feel great not only afterwards, but even while performing the task. Just the idea of cleaning something out can be fulfilling, since clearing out external clutter can reflect an emotional clearing or invite a physical cleanse. There's a joy to be found in living in an orderly manner—an order that reflects an increasing sense of internal harmony.

On the other hand, think about the times someone cleans out a closet and just loathes having to do it. It's the energy we bring to something that determines the quality of our experience.

I used to be the queen of turning a "get to," in the sense of having an opportunity to do something, into a "have to." At some point it became clear to me that being mindful to keep self-care on my "get to" list brings benefits beyond what I know to ask for.

The Source of Selfless Service

A great teacher of the Essenes, Dr. Beverly Gaard, shares an abundance prayer, "God is, I am, abundance: enough and to spare and to share for my every need now." This is the foundation for true, selfless service.

My niece Kristen has been delivering Meals on Wheels every Monday morning for many years. She doesn't do this from a place of burden, nor does she seek acknowledgment. She simply loves being of service from her own overflowing blessed life.

When Kristen's children are out of school for summer break or holidays, she takes them with her. When we visit, we go with her as well. She has a relationship with these individuals, and there's a reciprocal joy that happens with each interaction.

Our family was part of a coming of age ceremony for a friend last year. We were all asked to share about someone who inspires us. Of all the many individuals in my son's life, he shared about his aunt delivering meals on wheels. Kristen's sincere desire to be of service touched him deeply.

Kristen's basis for selfless service is gratitude for her life. She's aware of and grateful for the many blessings in her life. Gratitude creates an overflow of "enough and to spare and to share," and ignites the generosity of spirit we're all born with but that lies dormant in many of us.

There are also times when we don't feel particularly grateful, yet we still choose to give. Life's energy is circular. We give with no intention of receiving. Yet whenever we choose to give to another, we always receive back so much because the nature of giving is reciprocal.

Imagine the messages our children receive from us when they experience us enjoying service to others as a way of life.

20

How Good Can Your Life Be?

"**G**od has entrusted me with *myself*," said the Greek philosopher Epictetus.

My friend and yoga teacher Leigh Simran Brown illustrates this when she says, "Conscious breath after breath, intentional practice after practice, we till the field of our consciousness, creating a rich environment for our own growth and unfoldment. Set yourself up for full bloom. "

My intention as a mother is to be the best steward I can be of the precious life I have been entrusted with—that of my son. To do this well I must first be the best steward of my own precious life and the gifts I have been given.

Each and every one of us has been entrusted with our own precious life. We are here to cherish and treasure this life. Just as our children are, we are encoded with gifts and talents we have come here to share, contributing to those around us for as long as we are here. Becoming acquainted with our own unique gifts is the first step toward sharing them, for how can we share what we are unaware of or have lost touch with? Consequently, the more we thrive, the richer our caring for others can be, especially our children.

The more we mothers are fulfilled from within ourselves, the less we need our children to "be" or "do" anything in particular. Giving ourselves permission to live out our own life and dreams frees our children to be the exquisite individuals they too came here to be, living the life that they came here to live, free of a need to fulfill any abandoned dreams of ours.

I'm not suggesting that a mother needs to have dreams outside of the raising of her children. Many mothers I know are fulfilled by raising their children, since this is their dream, and being in their presence is a beautiful thing. I'm only suggesting that we, as mothers, need to be mindful that we don't unintentionally or unconsciously burden our children with anything that's incomplete in ourselves. The more fulfilled we are, the more we encourage our children to live lives that are unencumbered. Setting ourselves up for full bloom allows our children to do the same.

What's Holding You Back?

Have you ever wondered why, some people—and especially mothers—tend to settle at a certain level when it comes to the amount of good they experience in their life and specifically, in their family life? Not just in their material wealth, but in the quality of their relationships, and the sorts of experiences they have. Families exist at different strata, some high, some in the middle, and some low. So why, with exceptions, do we tend to gravitate to a certain level of existence?

When it comes to the good we feel we should receive in life, we all have what I think of as a set point—a picture inside of us of what we think is possible for ourselves as mothers and as a family, usually what we experienced in our family of origin. It's something inside us that functions rather like a thermostat, keeping us at the level we imagine we deserve. In actuality there's no limit to the amount of good there is in the universe, which means there's no reason any of us shouldn't enjoy a whole lot more of it, especially in our life as mothers and in the relationship with our children. Yet the fact is that some of us are able to receive and enjoy more good than others, and it's all because of what's occurring inside us.

Michael Beckwith tells the story of a bike ride he was taking a few years ago with a group of friends. They all started off together, but little by little Michael found himself lagging behind. This didn't make any sense. He's in great shape. He works out every day. His body is strong. He eats well. Still, he found himself continuously falling behind and consequently having to pedal harder. When they finally stopped and he got off his bike, he suddenly realized what the problem was—why he had to do so much "efforting" just to keep up. He had been riding with his brakes on and wasn't aware of it.

Do you see what I'm getting at? It doesn't matter how hard you work, how much effort you put out, how many goals you set for yourself, or how determined your intention is. If you have your internal brakes on in your life as a mother, nothing you do is going to give you the outcome you're hoping for. It isn't about effort, you see. It's about what you think is possible and how you *feel* about yourself, your life, and your relationship to the universe.

In a second analogy, place yourself inside a room from the Middle Ages, such as in a small shop in one of the ancient cities of Europe. The ceiling is perhaps six feet high at most. The doorways into the room are so low that an average person today has to stoop to enter. How does it feel to be in such a squashed space? Not too expansive, is it?

Now place yourself in a room with modern vaulted ceilings. Maybe the room has walls that are nine feet high, with the ceiling vaulted above this, and perhaps skylights. How does it feel now? It's akin to going to the mountaintop of our own consciousness, where there is no ceiling at all. The entire feel—our whole perspective—is transformed by the spaciousness.

If you want to raise the roof on the amount of good you personally can receive in your life, there's nothing better than self-care to assist you in doing so—and today, research confirms this. We now know that taking care of ourselves improves serotonin levels, making us feel good—and when we feel good, we bring good into our life without even trying.

When we feel good, we attract good.

We are infinite beings with enormous untapped space within us to experience ever-increasing good. Our potential, the unlimited possibilities within each of us, is unfathomable. The good feeling that comes from taking care of ourselves ignites the spark of passion, creativity, and inspiration within us to expand our life to its next level.

Mothers on a Mission

Especially for mothers, with others depending on us for so much, fulfilling our own unique destiny isn't always an easy task. Many mothers I work with have all but forgotten their dreams, tucking them away, intending to come back to them at some later time. However, I have found that no matter how deeply tucked away our dreams may be, there's a subtle—and sometimes perhaps not so subtle—unrest within us that begs for the sweet nectar a dream fulfilled brings into our life.

Regardless of how disconnected you may feel from the particular gifts that make you unique—the things that make your heart sing—they are truly just a choice away. With this in mind, over the next few days, consider inviting your forgotten gifts back into your life. This simple invitation often opens the floodgates for inspiration, ideas, creativity, and perhaps some long-forgotten purpose that's been neatly tucked away.

I have found that no matter how long a dream has been forgotten within us, there's a place just beneath the void we feel that knows exactly what we have come here to bring and longs to share our own unique gifts with those around us.

Sometimes our gifts can feel so much a part of who we are that it doesn't even occur to us that they are in fact gifts. However, when we look back at ourselves as we were as children, our gifts usually become glaringly obvious to us. Looking down from the mountaintop to our innocent and childlike self assists us in seeing ourselves in a way that perhaps we were unable to do at the time. We are usually able to see our natural inclinations, even if there wasn't anyone around to foster them or we felt we needed to hide them away. To this day, they remain deep within us, waiting in quiet repose for our return.

We each possess individuality and gifts that only we can contribute. In my experience, these gifts are easier to unearth when we're most relaxed, which is sometimes challenging when raising children. Nevertheless, I have observed that when clients are simply willing to reconnect, using self-care to make it a natural part of their day to do so, they discover that their gifts are more than eager to be given new life.

Rediscovering our gifts, dreams, and destiny doesn't need to take a lot of extra time and energy. Rather, as we saw earlier, the process actually brings us more time and more energy because our consciousness not only gets expanded so that it becomes spacious, but we find ourselves inspired, creative, joyful, and blissful.

You can reconnect with your "heart song" while you are in the shower, washing the dishes, taking a walk, or as part of your spiritual practice. You can bring it into a conversation with your children, assuming they are old enough to understand the context, when you are in the car with them on your way home from school or at the dinner table in the evenings. It's so enriching to our children to experience their parents reconnecting with their own interests and creating their own destiny. It's wonderful to model for our children that living on purpose is something we value. It teaches them that it's healthy to keep their own dreams alive—that it's for this that they were born. Do you see how this doesn't need to take time we don't have? We can choose to invest the time we do have in this conscious and inspiring way.

Remember, it's the *quality* of your life that *is* your life.

For mothers who are struggling just to make it through the day, discovering their dreams and their gifts can seem daunting at first. When you can't even imagine taking time for yourself given all the tasks you have on your plate, nourishing your spirit in this way may feel like an extravagance you can't afford.

I believe this process is meant to be easy, graceful, effortless, joyful, and even blissful because we are simply returning to something that already graces our being. If you take the steps I'm recommending, I promise you that reacquainting yourself with your gifts, your dreams, and your destiny will prove to be a rewarding journey.

Since it's practically impossible to fulfill your dreams from the paradigm of lack, guilt, and martyrdom, nourishing your spirit will assist you tremendously in this process. Inner-care moves you into the mindset of mutuality and abundance and reminds us there is more than enough for everyone to have their dreams fully lived. Living my dreams doesn't preclude you from living yours. In fact, it elevates the atmosphere between us and around us.

Shining your own light can't dim the light of others. The more light you shine, the more light you have to offer your children. When I think of some of the mothers I am working with currently, one is writing a children's book, a few are starting coaching practices for mothers—one for parents of special needs children and one for working mothers, one is considering a career change, one is considering having a third child, another is considering adopting a second child, one is running for public office, quite a few are navigating the worlds of work and family—and all of them are seeking to be the most conscious parent they can be. What they all have in common is that caring for themselves is directly benefitting their relationship with their children. Each one is experiencing a closer relationship with their children as they set themselves up for full bloom in their life.

The more mothers care for themselves, the more they have to offer, share and contribute to the world.

21

A Global Sisterhood of Thriving Mothers

I'm sometimes surprised by the level of judgment within the motherhood community. Working mothers feel judged, stay at home mothers feel judged, mothers of single children feel judged, mothers of special needs children feel judged, gay parents feel judged, mothers feel judged for their parenting choices, mothers feel judged by other mothers—the list goes on.

There's no better way to keep people powerless and disenfranchised than to have them fight with each other. When their energy is diffused rather than focused, they remain dispersed instead of bonded. For this reason it's imperative we talk about the ways that our judgements of each other keep us disempowered, because our true power and ultimate liberation comes when we join together collectively.

Whenever we find ourselves judging either ourselves or another mother, the root of such judgment is a sense of separation from one another. Mothers can feel like islands—and because we feel isolated instead of connected, we tend to objectify each other. This is what leads us to find fault.

We only ever judge another when we can't imagine what walking in their shoes feels like. If we could put ourselves in their position, we would see them very, very differently. But it goes deeper than a failure to understand another's situation. Let me remind you of what we saw earlier—that whenever we judge others, we are really judging *ourselves*.

As we have seen many times in the course of this book, our natural state is one of connectedness, which automatically breeds compassion. Judgment keeps people separate, whereas compassion brings them together.

Realizing we are all in this boat together, we begin to row in unison. We pull together, seeking to advance one another, in the recognition that when one person advances, the boat itself automatically advances.

Mothers Unite

Not only does judgment run counter to a mother's inherent nature, so also does competitiveness. Yet, especially in the workplace, there's often a great deal of competition among females, as with males.

Consider the unspoken sense that, given a position opening in the workplace, a woman without children is more likely to be asked to fill this position than a woman with children. It's presumed that a mother will be less available and therefore less effective than someone who has no children. Thus children are viewed as an impediment to a woman's success in the workplace. That being a mother with a family draws out many valuable qualities that can benefit a company is entirely in the shadow.

Anxiety, comparison, and competition, which are such predominant traits in many families, as well as in the business world as we know it today, come from a different mindset than being grounded in a sense that the universe provides for us abundantly. Wherever a competitive spirit prevails, it originates from a sense of lack. Feeling impoverished, which is rooted in the feeling that we ourselves are somehow lacking, creates a mindset of limitation and scarcity. This keeps us fearful, so that we are easily threatened by one another. It's at such times that we tend to mistakenly think we need to compete for what the other has or what we are afraid they may gain at our expense.

Once we learn to function from the realization that there's more than enough for everyone—plenty to go around for the whole of humankind—our experience of the world, and indeed of the universe, shifts dramatically. Thus the antidote to a competitive spirit is inclusivity. In this way, competitiveness and judgment are linked, since compassion fosters inclusivity. When you feel for someone, you naturally want to include them.

If a community is to be inclusive, it must begin with an internal inclusivity within ourselves. How this works is that when I include and embrace all the parts of myself, this naturally impacts how I behave in the external world. It becomes incongruent to judge or exclude others, no matter how different they may be from myself.

When I include and embrace all the parts of myself, I marvel at my own uniqueness. In this frame of mind, I'm able to receive the unique giftedness of other mothers around me. Because I give myself permission to shine as a mother, I see the gem other mothers are. When we recognize what gems we each are, it becomes obvious that there's no need to compete with one another—and even less need to judge and put one another down, since with our riches as individuals combined there's far more than enough to go around.

When you shine, it can't possibly take away from another person. To the contrary, not only does your shining inspire others to shine, but it illumines the treasure in the other.

To shine is attractive to the point of being contagious. Mothers will want what you've found. Whereas a sense of lack and limitation keep us fearful of one another and hence separate us, when we shine we bring one another together, uniting as a powerful collective. How can anyone feel disenfranchised, which is a state of weakness, if they know themselves to be one with all other mothers?

We are a global sisterhood, here to support and inspire each other. When one of us thrives, all of us benefit. We become a demonstration of the principle of abundance—that there is more than enough of everything to go around.

The world needs this message of abundance and plentitude. Mothers are the perfect vehicle to deliver the message. We must begin with each other, extend the message to our children, and together take it to the world.

A Walk in Her Sisters' Shoes

Stacy experienced what I'm talking about firsthand. A partner at a high-powered law firm in New York City, before she had children, she judged the mothers who worked at the firm as less effective. After all, how could they possibly work the hours she worked, with the commitment she displayed, when they not only had children to get home to but also had to respond to telephone calls from the school, attend doctors' appointments, and fulfill all the other duties of motherhood that sometimes take a mother away from the workplace for a time? She assumed that someone without children would do the job better.

Although never overt in her disdain, Stacy fell into the very mindset we have been describing. If she was up for a promotion alongside a working mother, she silently rolled her eyes. After all, a woman with children would leave the office earlier than herself to tend to her little ones, not to mention heading out the door if one of her children fell ill.

It wasn't until Stacy herself began to consider adopting that she became aware of just how judgmental she had been toward mothers. She realized she was afraid she would be passed over for partner and ultimately let go if she couldn't put in as many hours as her male coworkers. To follow her dream and become a mother exposed a vulnerability she had kept covered up for a long time. As she began the process of finding the courage to give life to her long silent dream, she realized just how threatened she felt.

It had been easier for Stacy to judge those mothers around her than face up to her fear and self-doubt. Now she had to address the difficult question of whether she could be a lawyer and also a mother, and do both well. Could she thrive as a mother with no family around her to help out? Could she maintain her standard of excellence and also nurture a child? If her life began to revolve around being a mother, might she lose her sense of purpose in her career?

As Stacy embraced these fearful elements of herself, she found herself reaching out to the very mothers she had until now judged. How did they perform well in their work while also managing to raise a child? She inquired into their experiences, sincerely interested in their insights. As she questioned and pondered their responses, she began to feel a closeness to these mothers, and even a camaraderie. She was amazed at the amount of support she received—so much so that she initiated the daunting process of adoption.

Stacy ultimately adopted two precious children, and to this day the mothers around her at work are still an important part of her support system, not to mention an inspiration. They are a mutual admiration society. Stacy learned that there's more than enough for all of them to thrive, and that by joining together as a collective they were far more empowered than they were as individuals.

Because Stacy had the courage to reach out to the very individuals she had judged, through their connection she discovered gifts she never imagined possible. Where there had been only criticism and competitiveness, today there is a thriving community.

There are so many ways to mother, and mothers have so many gifts to share with their families, each other, and the world.

22

Living in the House of Tomorrow

The greatest joy any of us can experience is *to be the cause of joy for another person.* So said the great American psychologist Marshall Rosenberg, creator of Nonviolent Communication.

We can even go further and state that we truly experience our own fullness of joy when our actions inspire the inherent joy at the heart of others. So if we are given a tremendous idea, have a certain creative gift, or make a wonderful discovery, it's meant to bless us *as we use it to be a blessing to others.*

It has become abundantly clear to me that to be a cause of joy for another isn't something alien to our nature, but is our nature in its most authentic expression—and I have seen this so beautifully demonstrated in my own son.

My husband Jami and I lead transformational travel trips around the world. Last year we took a group to Bali. I marveled as I watched our son William, eleven years old at the time and still so connected with this natural state, untouched by the sense of lack that's so pervasive in our culture and drives our extreme materialism.

While in Bali, we visited some of the local marketplaces in which artisans make and sell their exquisite work. William noticed how the tourists around him were trying to bargain down the local people to get a cheaper price for their goods. He remarked to me, "Mom, I don't understand it. Everyone is trying to pay them less, but everything here already costs way less here than it does at home. And the people here don't have a lot of money. Why would we do that? I'm going to do the opposite. I'm going to give them *more* than what they ask for. So if they tell me it's 50,000 rupiah, I'm going to give them 100,000 rupiah instead." He took such delight in offering more than what was being asked of him, doubling it in fact—$10 instead of $5.

Observing the look on the faces of these beautiful Balinese artisans and the connection they made with my son took my breath away. Such humanity! William is representative of children who are still connected to their innate sense of generosity and abundance. Generosity comes partly from knowing there's enough, but also from knowing that *we* are enough. William was living from an inner space of abundance, not lack— in other words, from his natural state.

Thriving is Contagious

There has never been a more important time in history for those of us who mother to step into our individual and collective authentic power. In contrast to how society has tended to see us, and consequently we have seen ourselves, we mothers are coded and encoded to contribute to the world, especially through the raising of our children. In fact, because we are hardwired to share our gifts, we have an actual *need* to do so in order to feel fulfilled. I've learned that none of us ever truly rest until we are giving the gifts we have come here to give and living the life we have come here to live.

Today, we mothers have an unparalleled opportunity to bring our female gifts of connection, relationship, intuition, and feminine authority to the workplace as well as the family. It's our time to take ownership of our native gifts and cultivate them as both valuable and essential for the advancement of society.

When we witness someone sharing their gifts out of a feeling of overflowing fullness and therefore living with purpose, it's so attractive that it inspires us to do the same in our life. It actually expands our consciousness to witness another mother being true to herself.

Beyond attractive, it's positively contagious! The vitality, the sheer aliveness, reminds us of our need to share our own giftedness. In this way, our self-giving inspires others to give of themselves in the same authentic manner—our children, our friends, our colleagues at work, and indeed everyone whose life we touch, spiraling out and changing the world.

I want to emphasize that this can begin in the simplest of ways. To illustrate, a client of mine decided to reconnect with a love of sewing that she had enjoyed as a child but put away once she herself had children. How often, when a woman becomes a mother, does all of the activity of raising a child eclipse who the mother is herself?

As my client reconnected with her creativity, she initially sewed costumes for the plays at her son's school. In time, with so many costumes, they needed to find an outlet for their extras. They found a school in need, began donating their extra costumes and ended up building a bridge between the two schools. As children got to know each other and went to see each other's plays, the effect began to ripple out beyond the initial gesture. Two communities were being enriched, their lives joined together in a creative and caring venture, all because my client began to awaken to a vital aspect of herself that had been lost in the mists of raising her children.

It's important to point out that this wasn't a case of a mother filling a need that had arisen in the local community. Many mothers do this kind of thing, but this too can come from feeling guilt over "not doing enough to help," rather than flowing from the mother's own center. It's vital to access the essence of who we are so that we don't end up just multiplying our "doing," but are actually coming from being true to who we are. It's a matter not of merely helping out, but of knowing our value—identifying what we love to do—and allowing this to become our channel of service.

The joy that my client experiences when sewing and sharing her beautiful costumes is positively contagious!

The Spiritual Authority of Motherhood

So different is a thriving mother's world, with its consequent effect on how her children grow up and the impact those children then have on the world around them, that for mothers to thrive as individuals *is* to change the world.

When mothers value ourselves, we model for our children that each person is important—that their being here on this earth matters.

Individuals who value themselves aren't afraid to show up for the magnificent people they are, and consequently they transform society.

Mothers are here to be seen, not to be largely invisible other than on occasions such as Mother's Day.

We mothers are an untapped spiritual powerhouse on the planet. We have within us qualities desperately needed at this time in our history. As pointed out earlier, I'm talking about qualities that give us a unique spiritual authority that comes from our *being*—such qualities as our own inner spiritual connection, the ability to connect deeply with others, to relate intimately, to process matters, to nurture, to draw on a mother's intuition, and to express the kind of female caring one sees in a mother bear protecting her cubs.

To live a life in which we thrive because we are connected to our deepest being is so different from operating out of the burdened mindset of seeking to please others. Attempting to keep everyone happy is a martyred state of frantic "doing."

The spiritual teacher Amma, or Mother, known as the Hugging Saint, states "the forthcoming age should be dedicated to awakening universal motherhood. This is crucially important. The future of humanity lies in the hands of women. Women everywhere have to actualize the qualities of motherhood within themselves. This is the only way to realize our dream of peace and harmony in the world, and to further progress in life."

For how many generations have mothers struggled just to make it through the day, so they couldn't possibly think about changing the world? You can't change the world if you are in survival mode.

The Spiral of Connection

This is our time as mothers to restore our connection to our authentic self, to connect with our children, and to join together as a global world in which we all thrive. As Amma put it, women everywhere need to *actualize* the qualities of motherhood within themselves.

We must first individually embody the consciousness of our own inner fulfillment. Then we must declare, "I can make a difference by connecting with other mothers across the planet." Because form follows consciousness, the result will be a transformation of the planet that ultimately renews the entire Earth.

So how do we go about forming a global connection among mothers?

Our connection to one another takes the shape of a spiral. When we first reconnect with ourselves, getting in touch with our authentic nature, it creates an inner fountain, which produces an overflow. Any real connection with others originates in this inner awakening and wellspring.

It simply isn't possible to experience our inner connection to the infinite, inexhaustible presence that's the essence of all life and not find this flowing spontaneously into all our relationships. We experience meaningful connections with our children, our spouse, our friends.

We also begin to connect with our giftedness—our talents. These then impact such aspects of our life as our creativity, the work we engage in, and our finances. They become tools we use in shaping a vision for humanity—our own humanity first, that of our children next, and ultimately the humanity of the whole world.

Connect with yourself and you will automatically find your connection with your children enriched. This inner connectivity will then flow spontaneously out to those you don't even know personally. In whatever way works for you, you'll quite naturally find yourself becoming a philanthropist and making a difference to the lives of others. As more and more of us join with others in this effortless way, we will create a potent collective consciousness, powerful enough to uplift the vibration of the world.

A New Vision of Motherhood

Does the idea that mothers can actually transform the world sound far-fetched, even impossible? On the contrary, that motherhood is the power that can change the way we function as human beings is as natural as breathing.

You might ask why, if it's so natural, why hasn't it happened yet. My answer is that it's for the simple reason that motherhood has never been valued and has been defined for us by others. Society has dictated what a mother is and what a mother does, and we have bought into it. I love the vision I spoke of earlier in the book of mothers as philanthropists, with more than enough to share freely and to empower others from our natural state of overflow.

When a mother who lives in Kansas thrives, and another in New York does also, then we add to these a mother in Zimbabwe, along with one in Canada, and yet another in Australia, and we connect these mothers with each other as thriving individuals, collectively they become more than the sum of their parts. They begin to define what it is not only to be a thriving mother, but what it means to be a spiritually connected being living out our fullest potential.

When my husband and I saw the movie *Selma*, I was so moved by the scene in which Martin Luther King, Jr. is at the White House asking LBJ to order the federal government to step up their efforts to grant voting rights to African Americans. Johnson told King that it wasn't a priority for his administration that year and would have to wait until the following year's legislative session. Dr. King responded that there was no question of waiting another year, for people's rights were being violated *now*. If the federal government wouldn't help, they would continue with marches and peaceful demonstrations. The lesson is that Martin Luther King didn't wait for the world to recognize his vision. Instead he brought his vision to the world.

I have a vision of mothers thriving, united, and joined collectively around the globe. This can be accomplished by a group of individual mothers who are dedicated to the value of their own wisdom rather than to the popular, trendy, oppressive, and limiting definition of our surrounding culture. As Margaret Mead said, "Never doubt that a small group of thoughtful, committed citizens can change the world; indeed, it's the only thing that ever has." Evolving the planet one thriving mother at a time, such women can ignite a global movement of higher consciousness.

Of this I am absolutely certain. Connect thriving mothers from every corner of the planet and we'll end all war. Connect mothers with a purpose from all corners of the planet and we will ensure that our children thrive and our planet thrives along with us.

The time is now for mothers to value ourselves, to step into our inestimable worth, and to form global connections. We have no time to waste because our children are here *now*, needing to experience their own worth and value. Their future is now. And, as my son William said in the lyrics of a song he composed, speaking of this particular time in world history into which he has been born, "I want to leave it better than I found it." Our children naturally want to make a difference.

We mothers are here to *show* society that we are here now. We are here to be seen, heard, valued. We have so much to offer, so much in which we can make a difference and become the inspired humans we have the potential to be.

To conclude, I'd like to share with you the lyrics of the song I just mentioned, which was composed by my son William for the Los Angeles Green Festival when he was eleven and won first place.

Open Up Our Eyes
It's time to open up our eyes
before another creature dies
It's time to spread our wings and fly
Leave the ground behind

I see solutions
to the pollution
My generation
Will change the nation

I'm only sayin
what I been prayin
we work together
change this world forever

It's time to open up our eyes
before another creature dies
It's time to spread our wings and fly
Leave the ground behind

I feel unruly
Think it's my duty
To make a difference
In this world of beauty

You're asking questions
I'm giving answers
I wanna leave here
better than I found it

It's time to open up our eyes
before another creature dies
It's time to spread our wings and fly
Leave the ground behind

FULL CIRCLE MOMENT

On Mother's Day, I received a handmade card from my son. In it he said:

You are <u>the best</u> mom <u>ever</u>! You are <u>always</u> there for me, and I hope I can always be there for you! I'm <u>so</u> glad that we are <u>so close</u> and I'm <u>grateful</u> that we can do <u>anything</u> together! I love you <u>so</u> much!

This was written by the same boy who told me I was too serious and needed to smile more. Same boy, different mom.

I'm so glad I listened to him. In just nine short months I gave birth to a new "me."

I learned that when I take care of myself, my child is the beneficiary. I discovered that we must do whatever it takes to care first and foremost for our own spirit, which is at the heart of our lives—physical, mental, emotional and spiritual. Our own transformation is the greatest gift we can give our children, freeing them to be themselves.

Dear Mom,
   You are <u>the best</u> Mom <u>ever</u>!
y
You are <u>always</u> there for me, and
I hope I can <u>always</u> be there for
you! I'm <u>so</u> glad that we are <u>so</u>
<u>close</u> and I'm <u>greatful</u> that we
can do <u>anything</u> together! /Love,
   I love <u>you so</u> much! /Will

Made in the USA
Columbia, SC
18 October 2022

69701393R00114